Bruno Ruviaro

Pós-Tudos

12 etudes for piano solo

Oakland, California, 2016

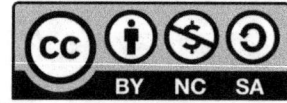

About this work

These twelve piano etudes were composed between Summer of 2015 and Fall of 2016 in San Francisco and Oakland, California. The word *Pós-Tudo* comes from the poem of same name by Augusto de Campos. For a long time I had intended to compose a series of piano pieces based on the borrowing and transformation of existing musical material. This collection is a realization of that idea. The main source material of each etude is cited at the bottom of its last page. Other fleeting appearances of borrowed music are referenced directly on the score. Half of the sources are popular songs (mostly Brazilian music); the other half comes from Western concert music tradition. This collection of *Pós-Tudos* brings together ideas, sounds, and gestures that have been slowly cooking for over two decades of my music making.

Many thanks to my pianist friends and colleagues, past and present, for directly or indirectly inspiring me to create these pieces; Santa Clara University and the Department of Music for giving me space, time, and material conditions; Kyle Adam Blair for the first studio recording and public performance; and thanks to Tania and Pira for enduring my non-stop banging on the piano for months in a row.

Bruno Ruviaro

Glossary of Portuguese terms

Bem barulhento – Very noisy

Pouquíssimo pedal, ad lib. – Very little pedal, ad libitum

Tempo ondulante, sempre rubato – Fluctuating tempo, always rubato

Trocar devagar durante a fermata – Change slowly during fermata

Um pouco mais lento se precisar – A bit slower if needed

TABLE OF CONTENTS

Engraved with Lilypond - http://lilypond.org/

Pós-Tudo 1

para Joana Cunha de Holanda

Bruno Ruviaro

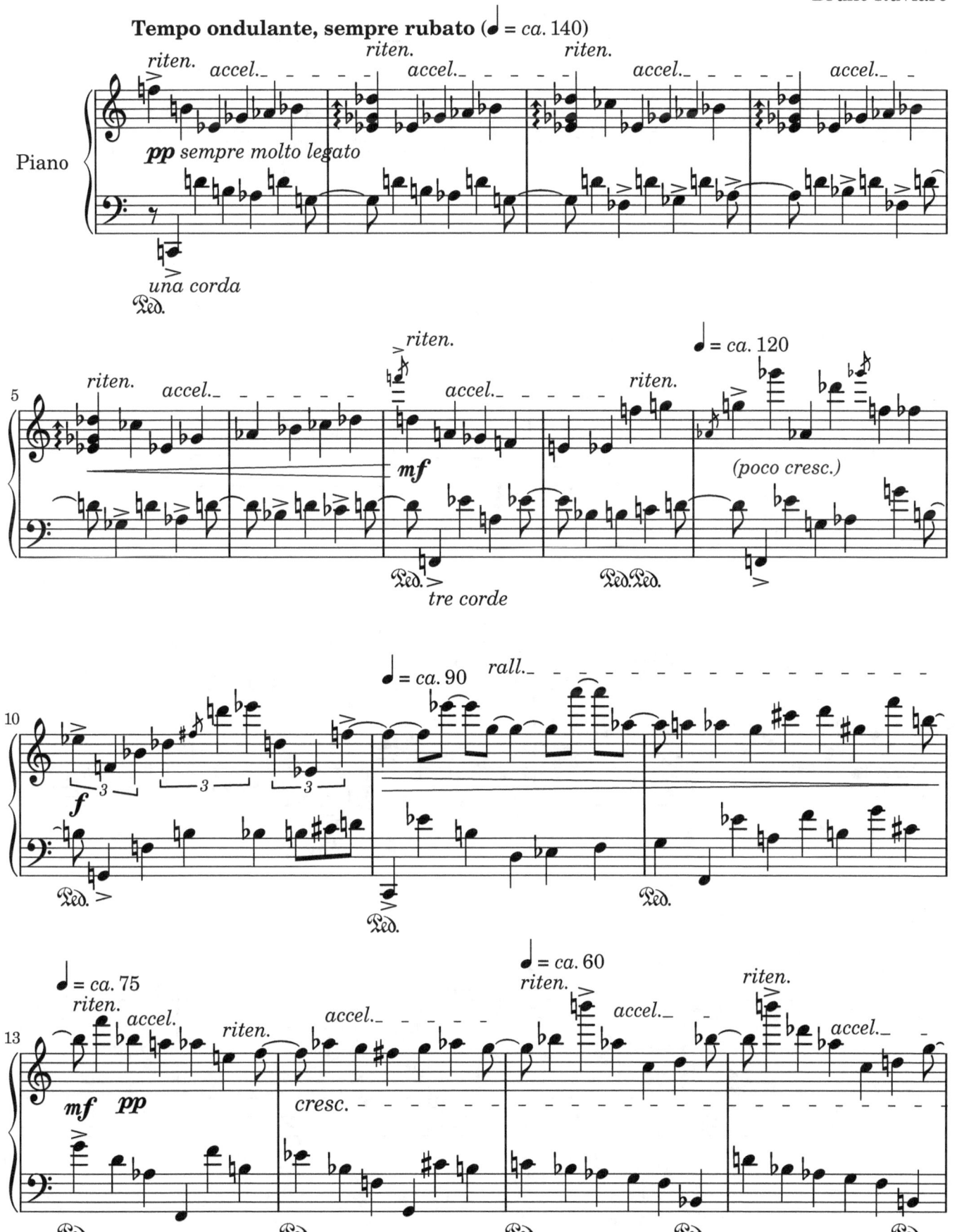

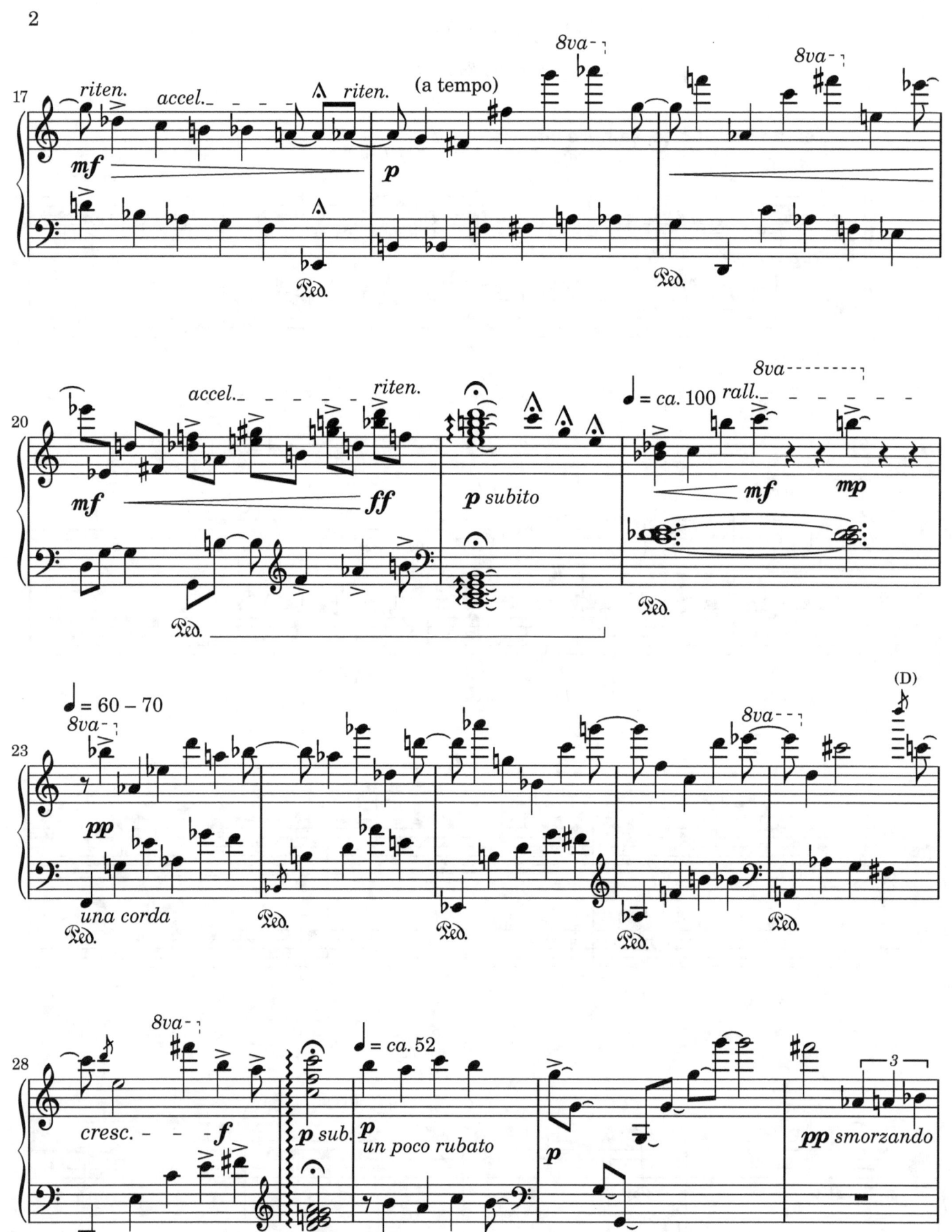

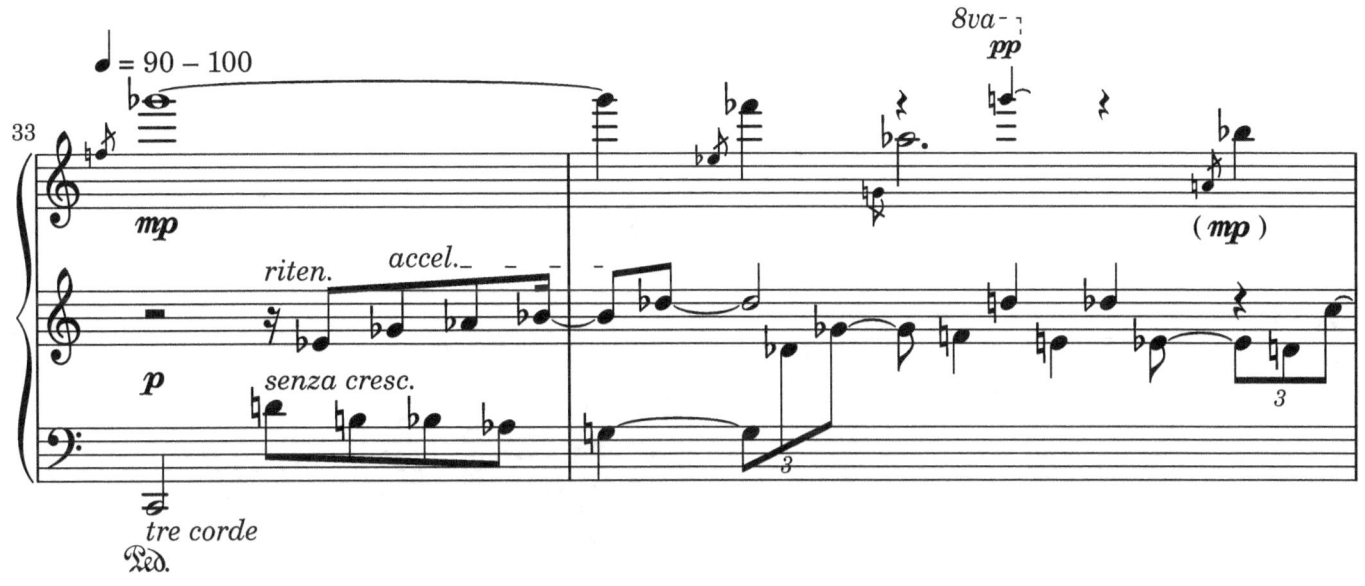

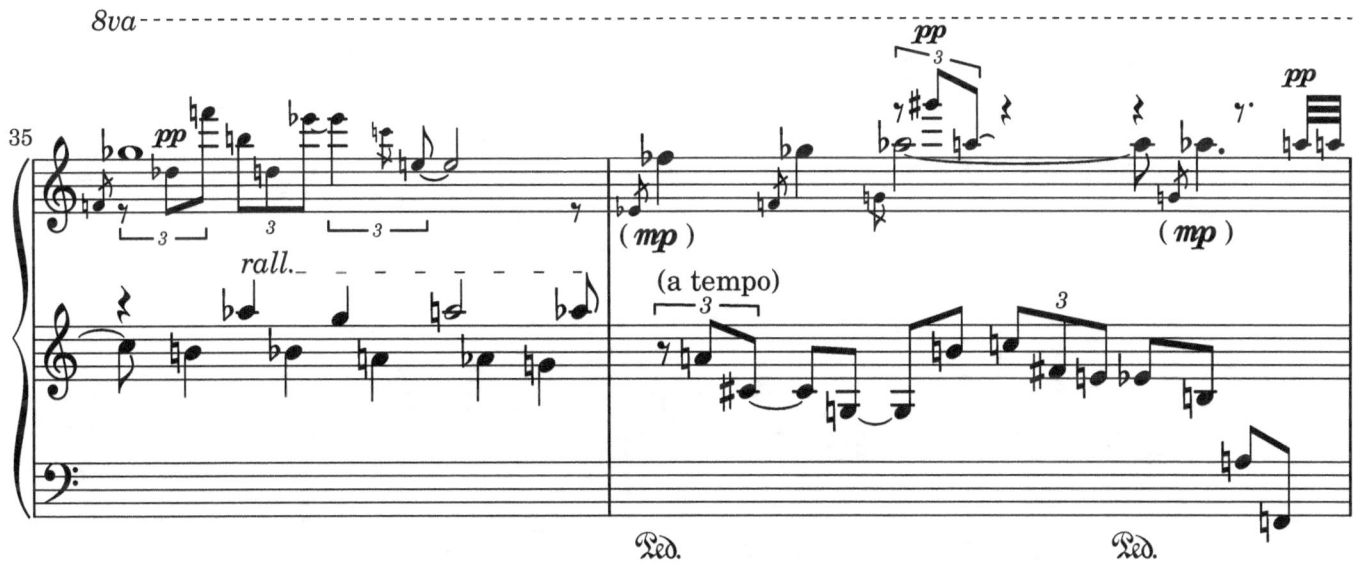

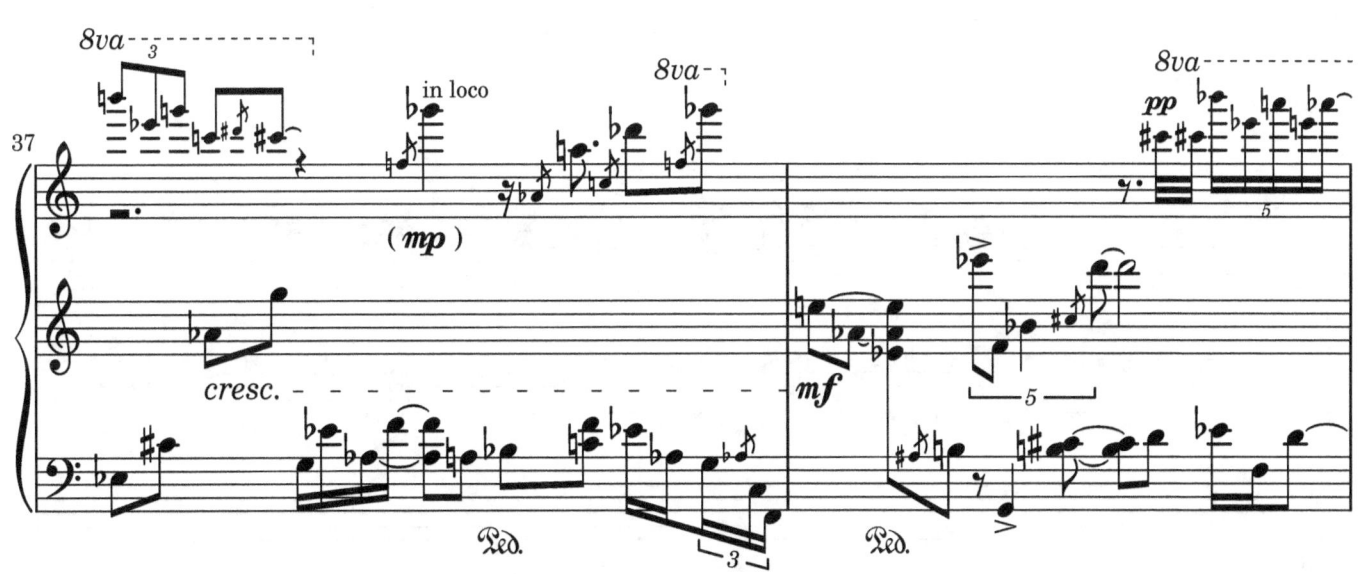

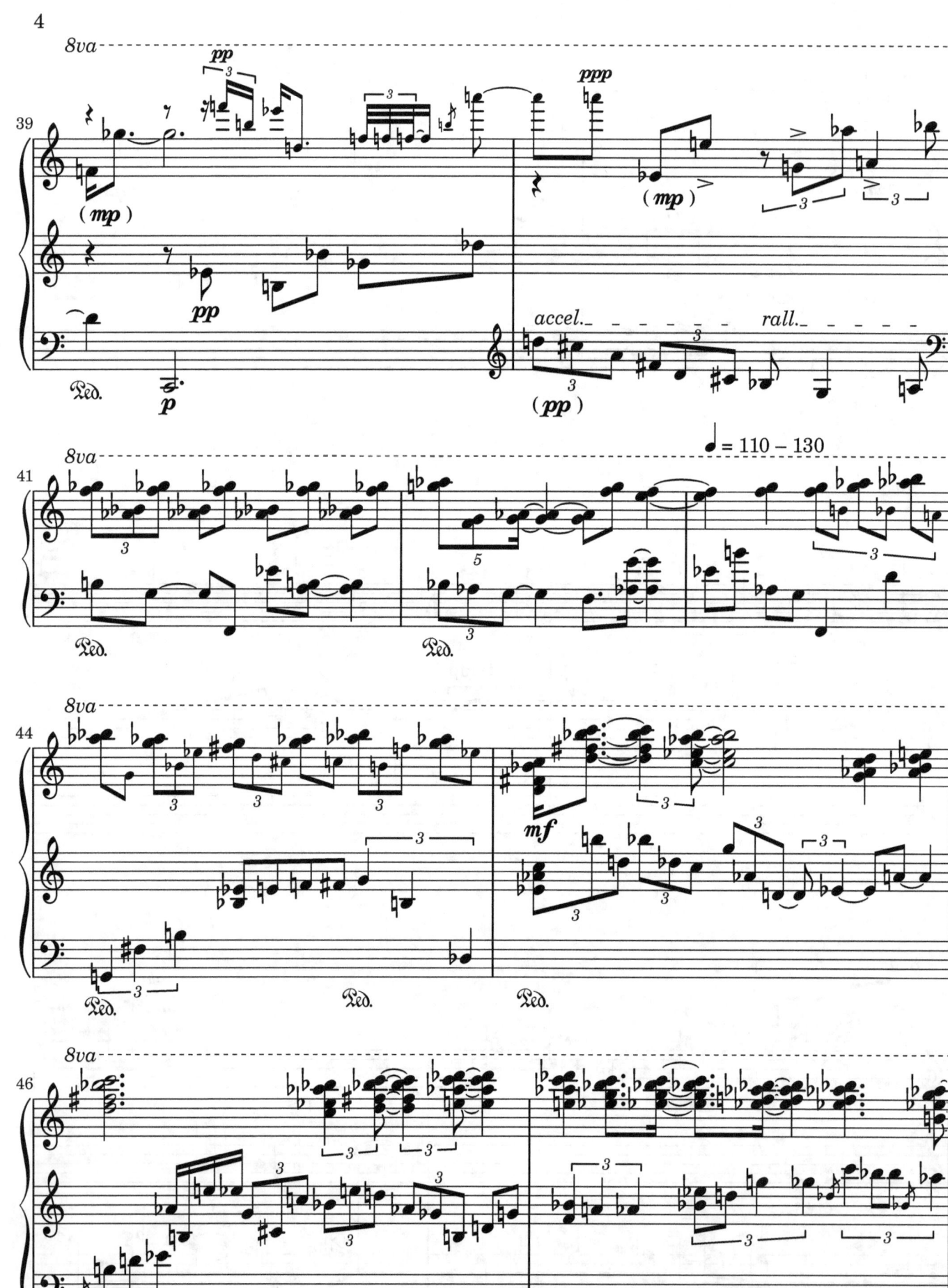

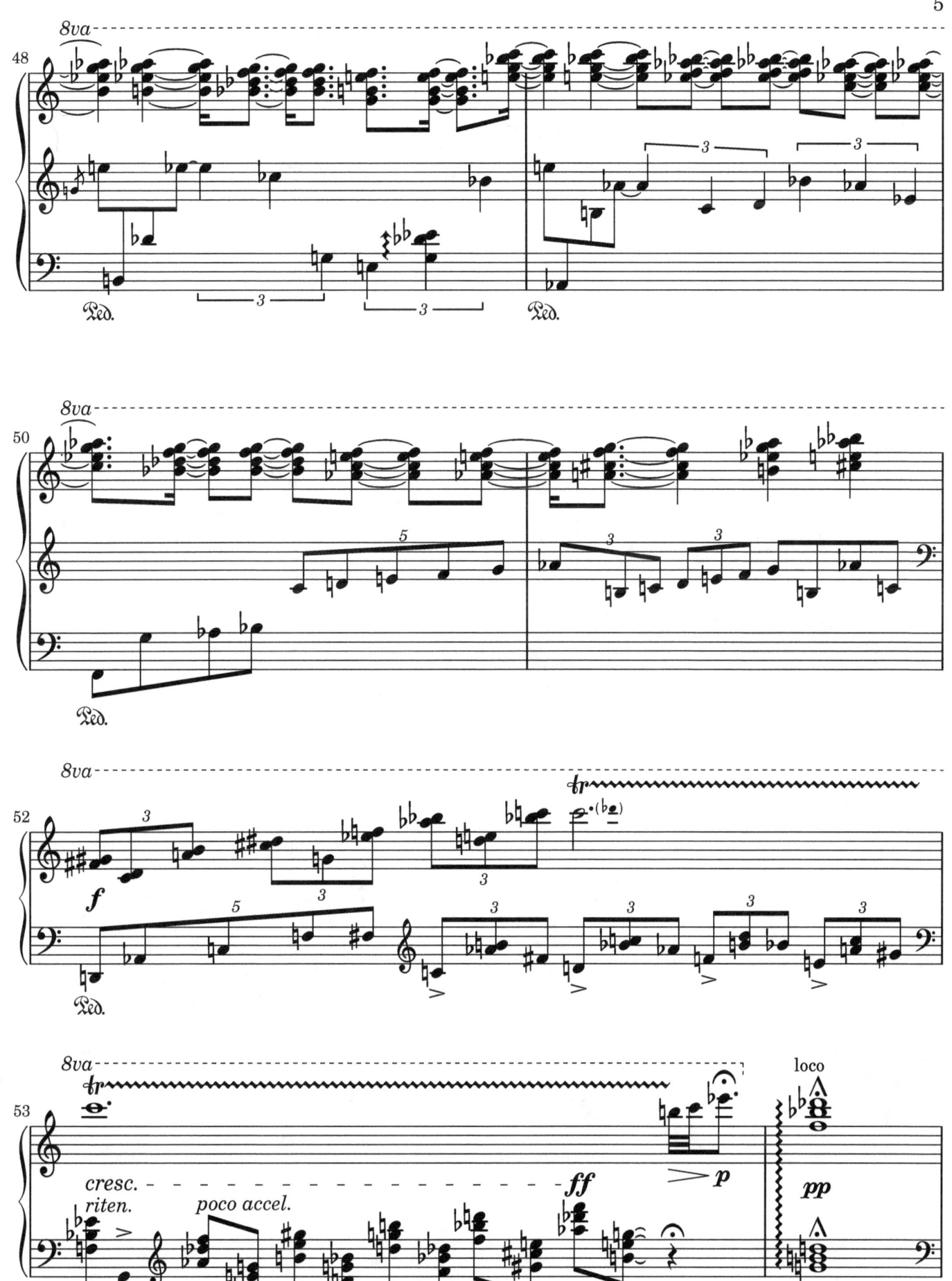

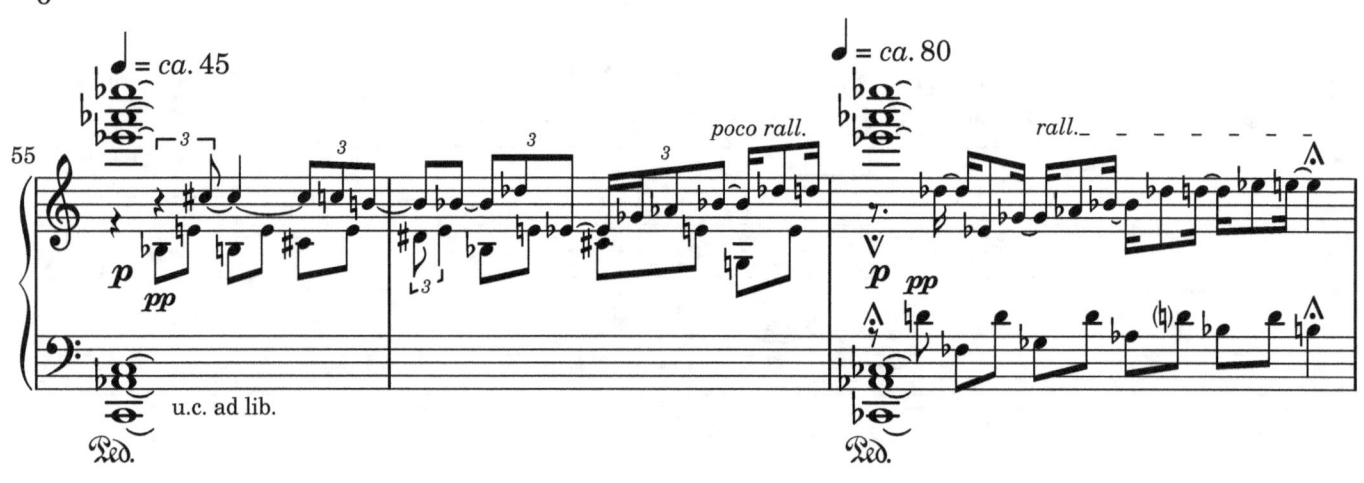

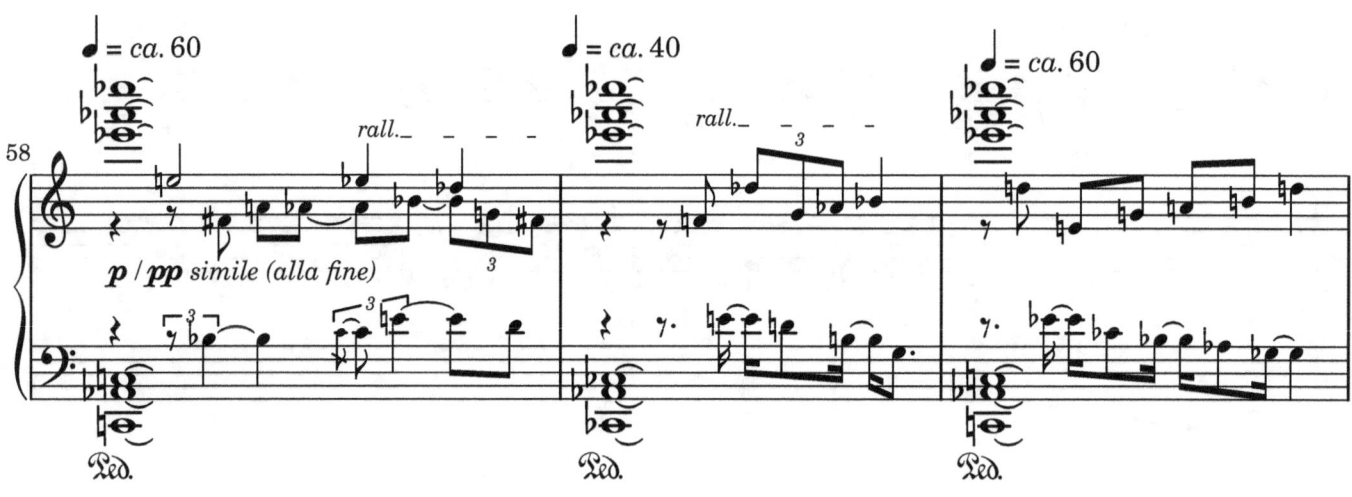

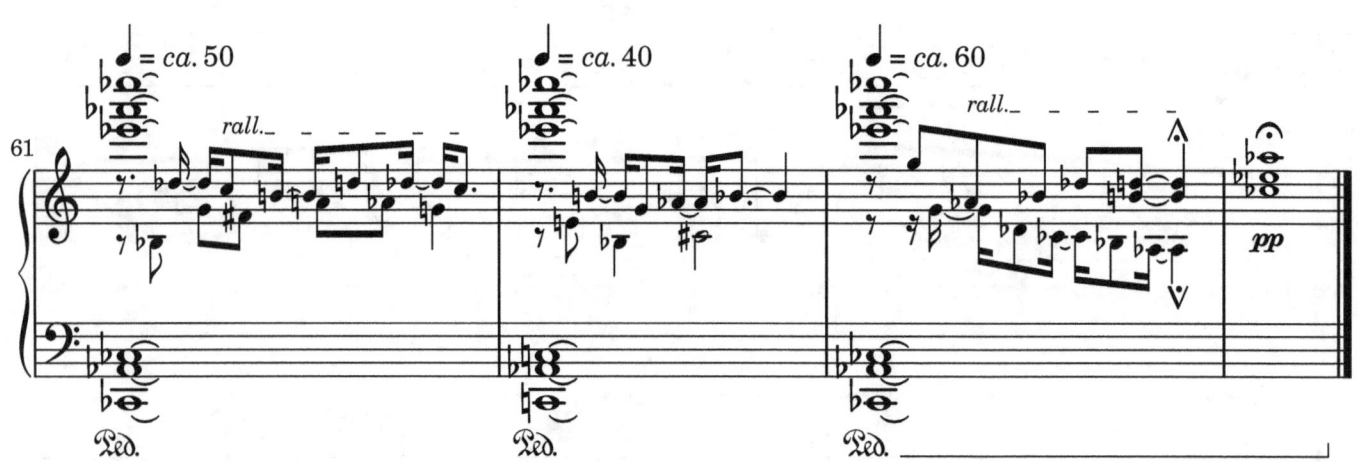

[*Luiza*, Tom Jobim]

Pós-Tudo 2

para Carina Joly

Bruno Ruviaro

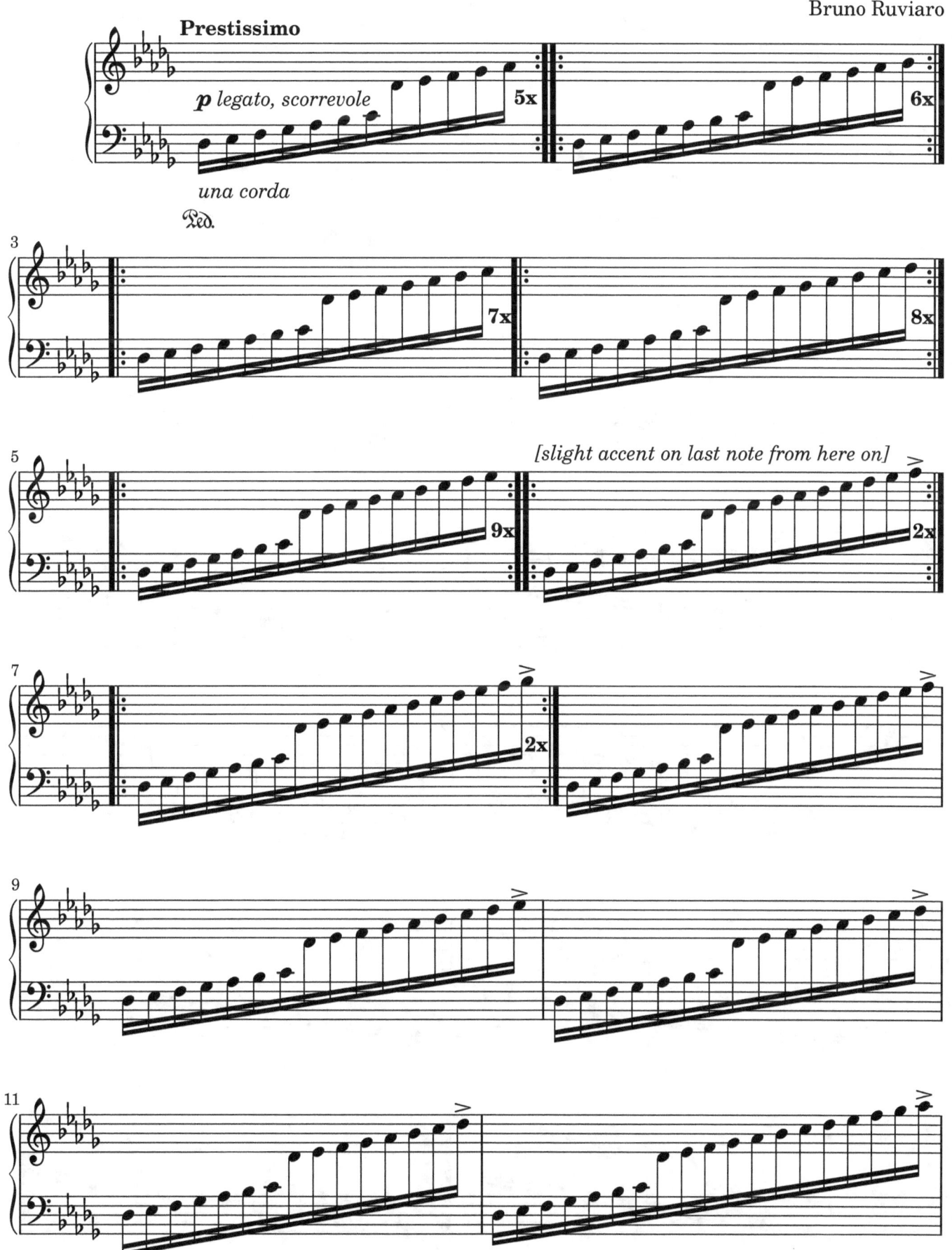

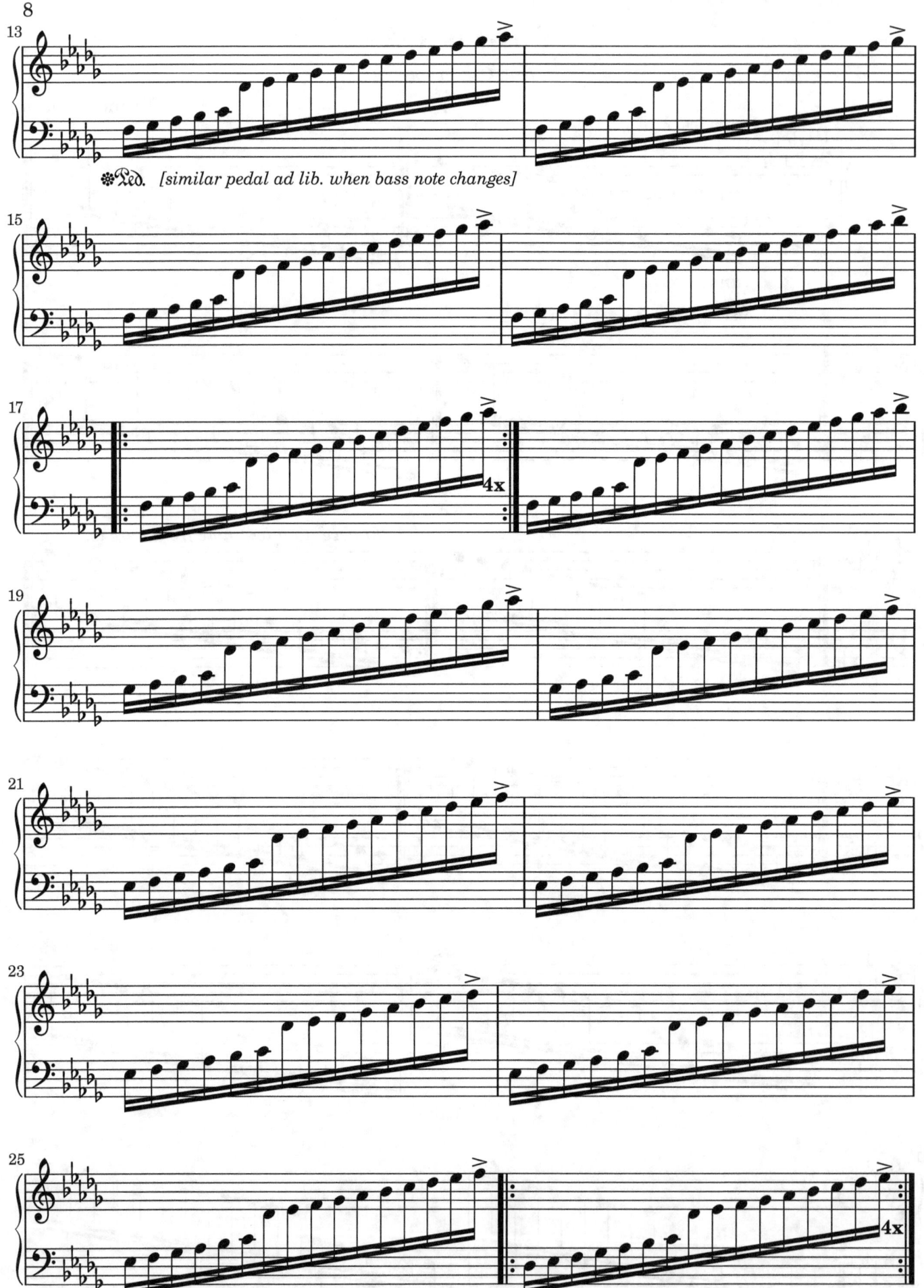

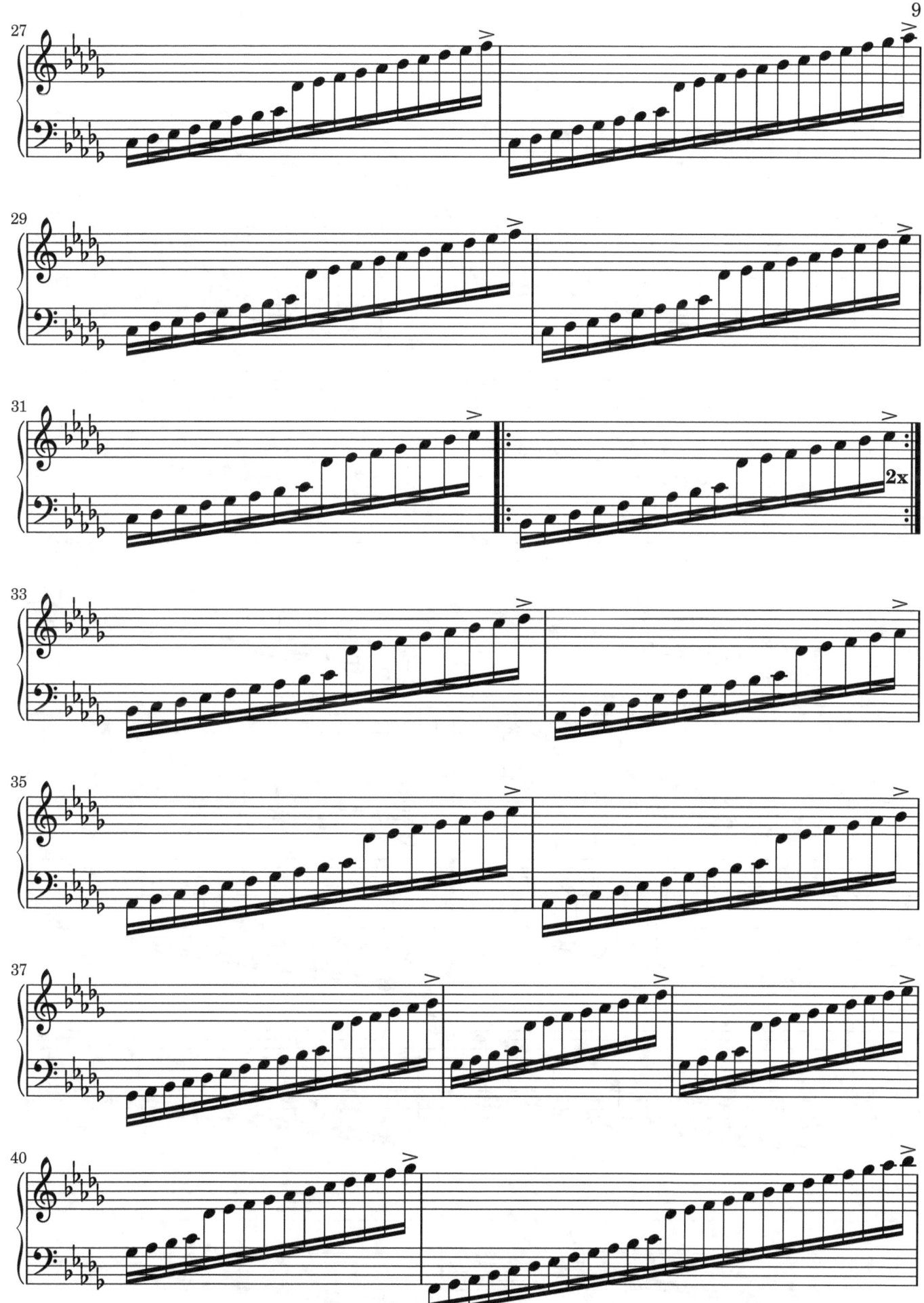

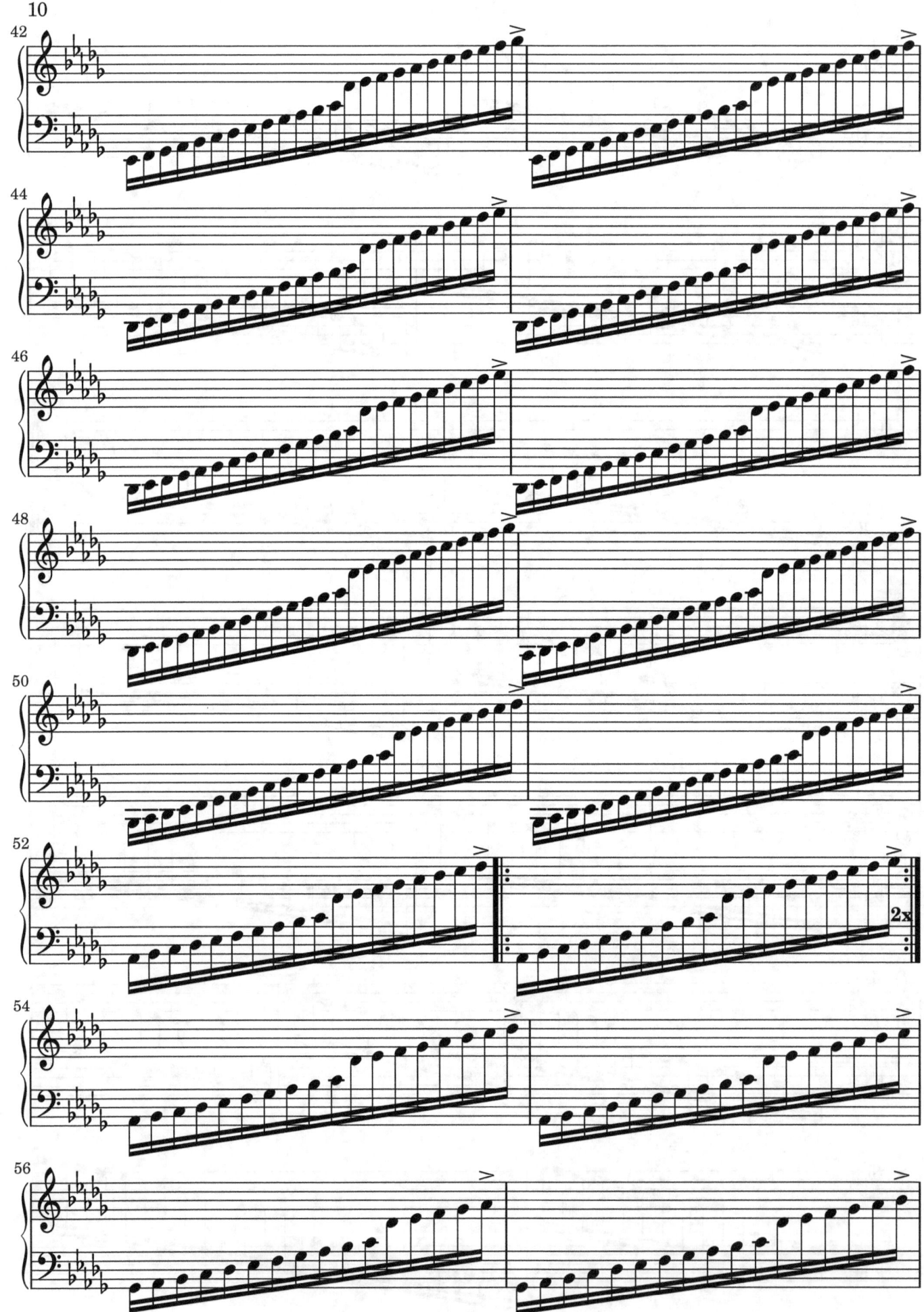

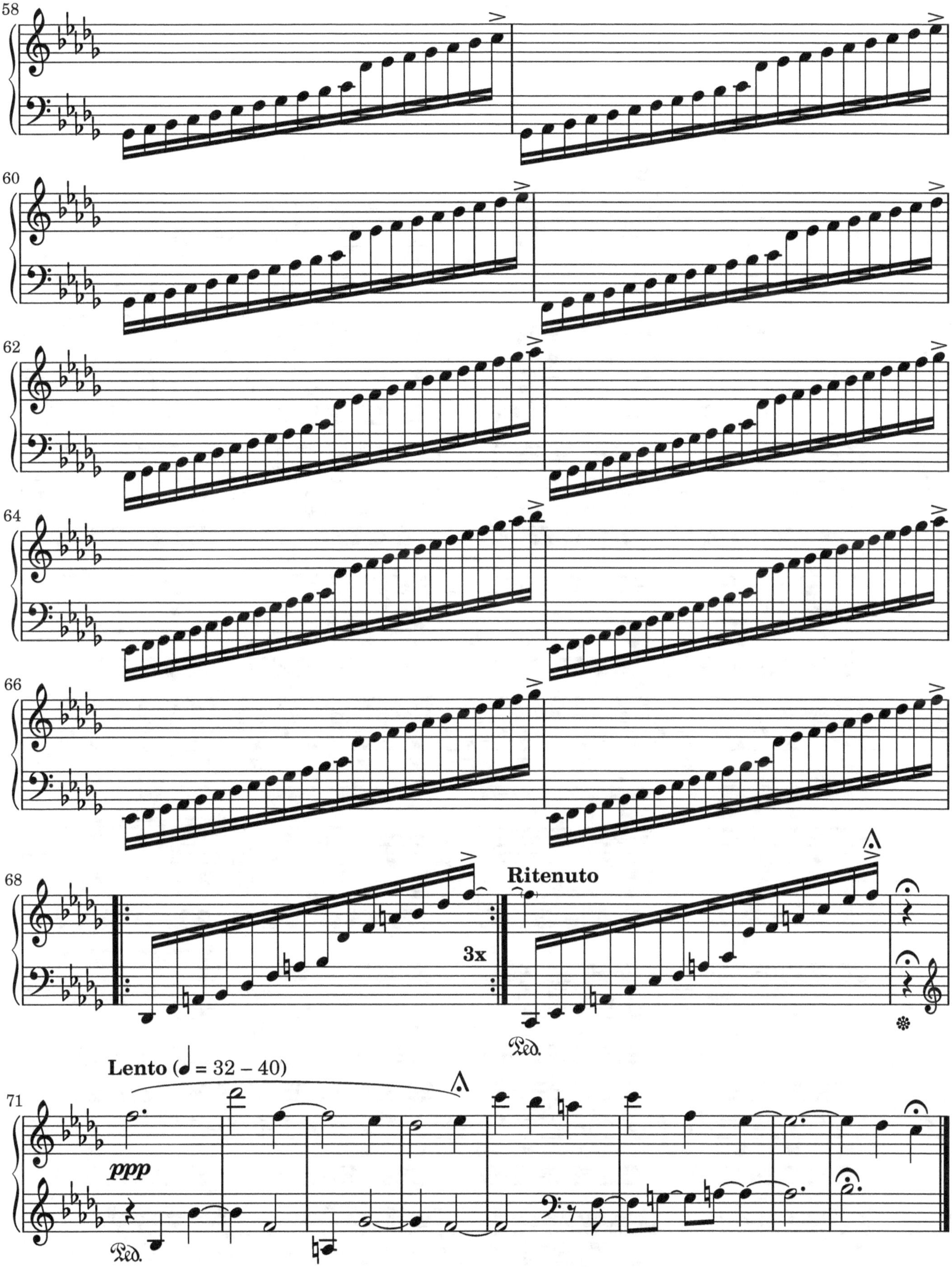

[*2nd movement from piano concerto in G, Ravel*]

Pós-Tudo 3

Bruno Ruviaro

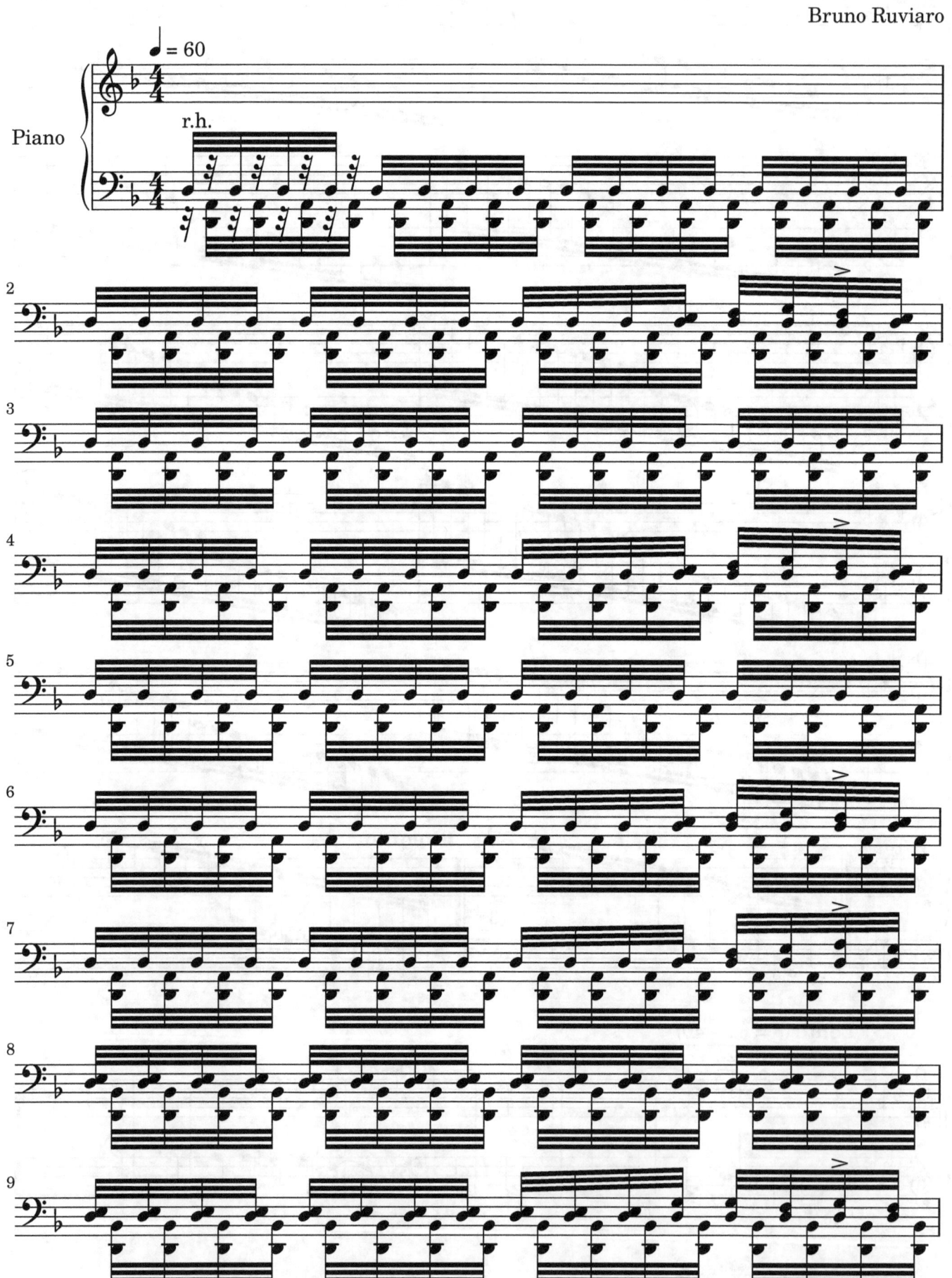

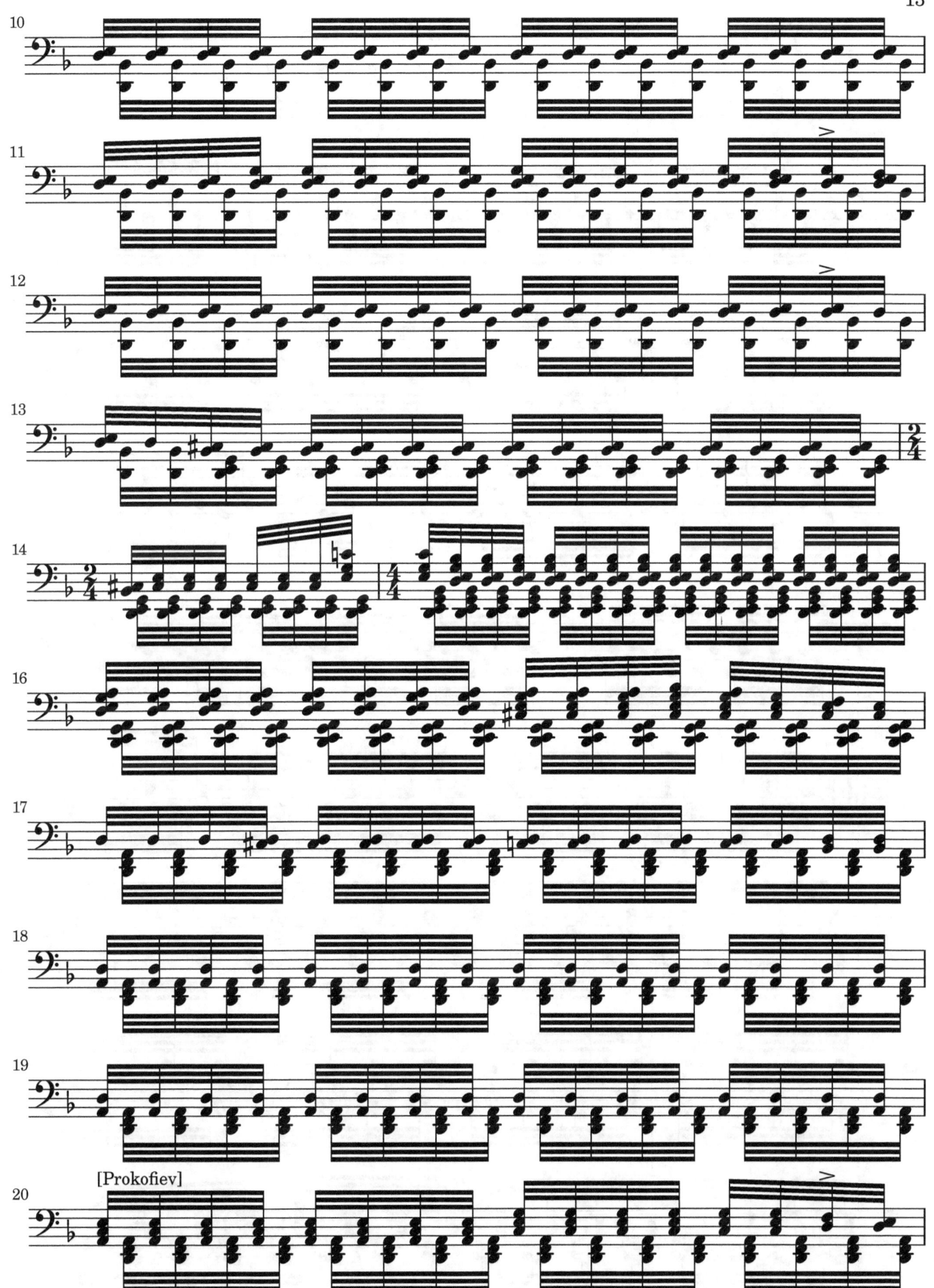

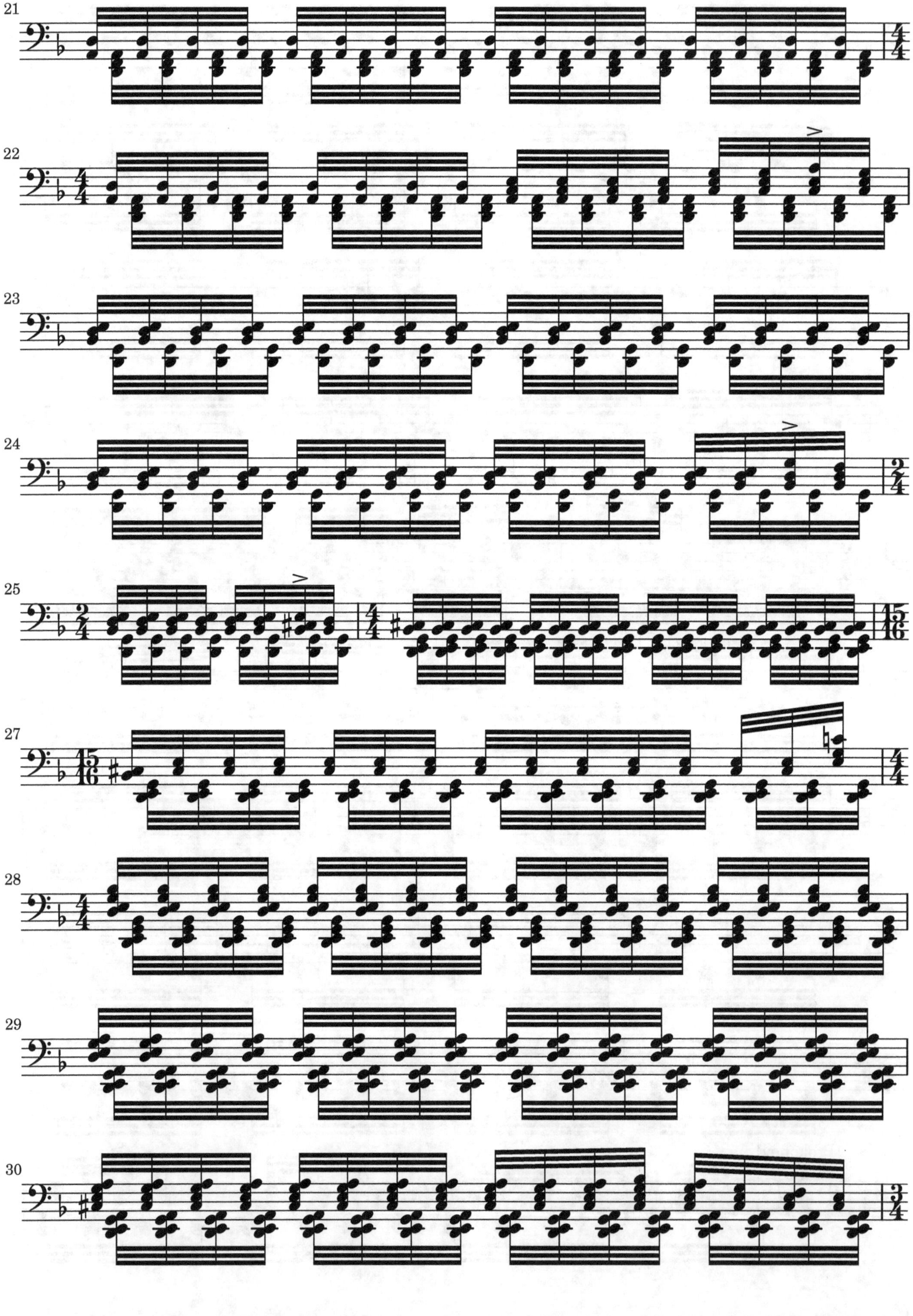
21
22
23
24
25
27
28
29
30

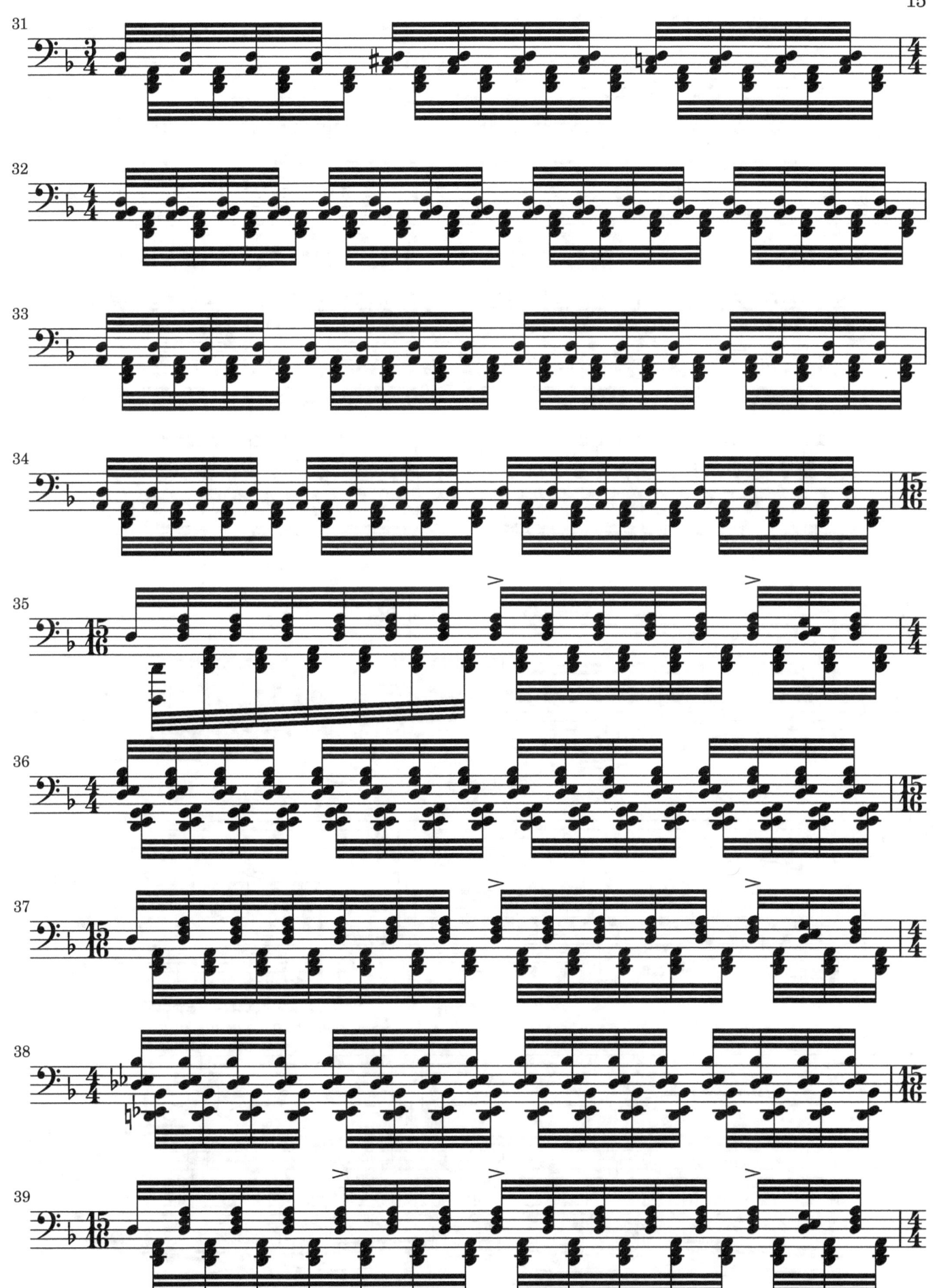

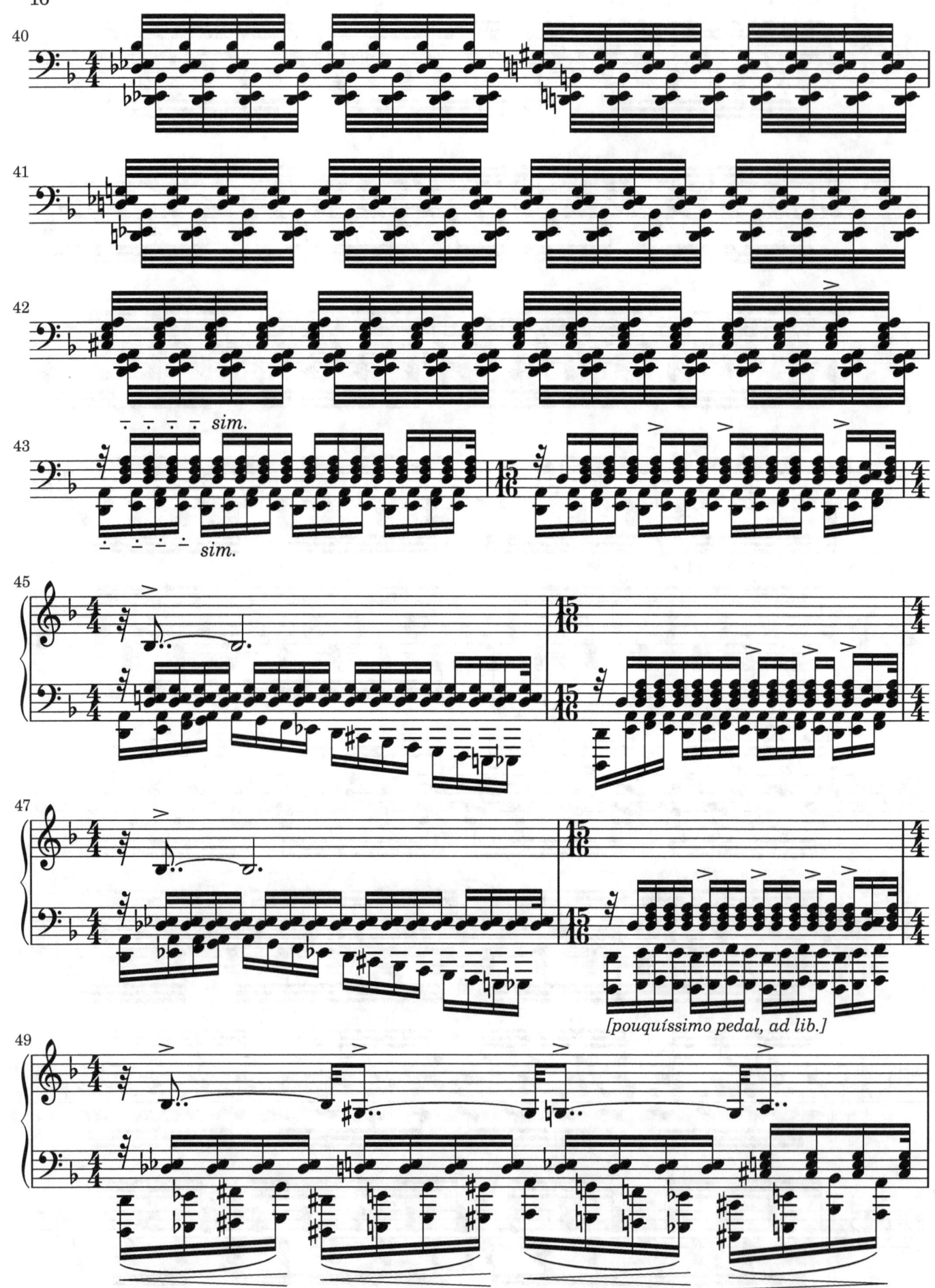

[pouquíssimo pedal, ad lib.]

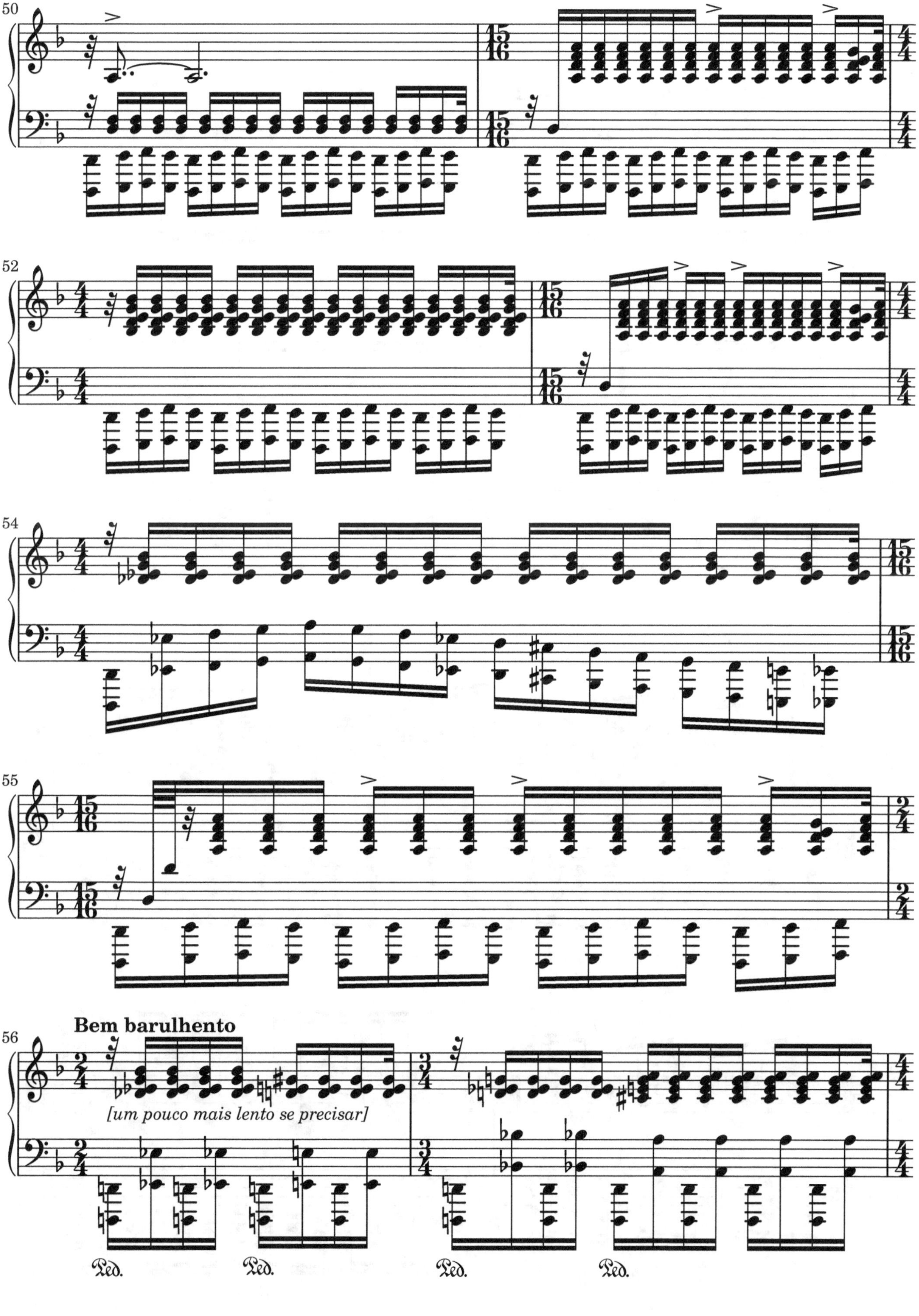

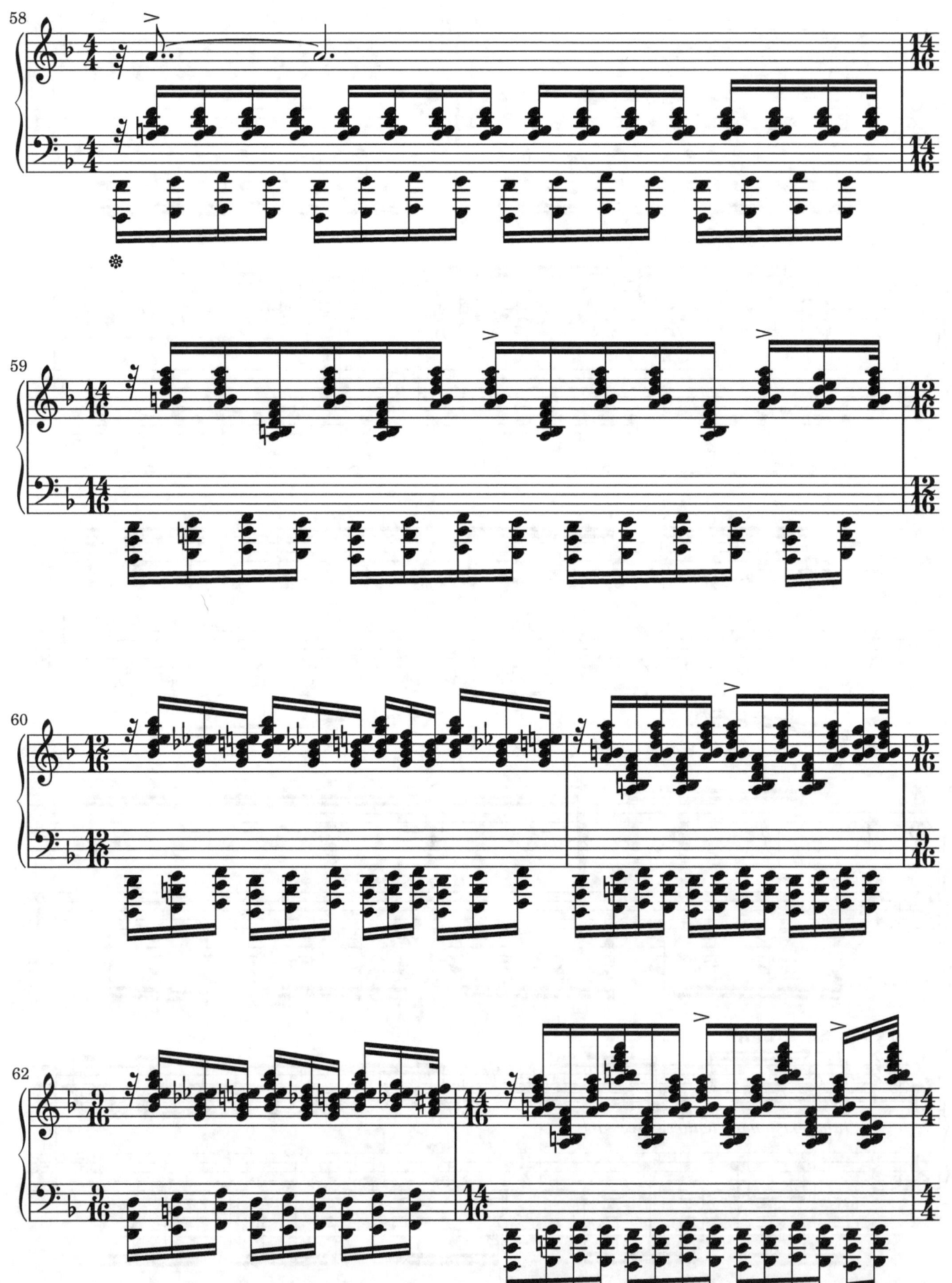

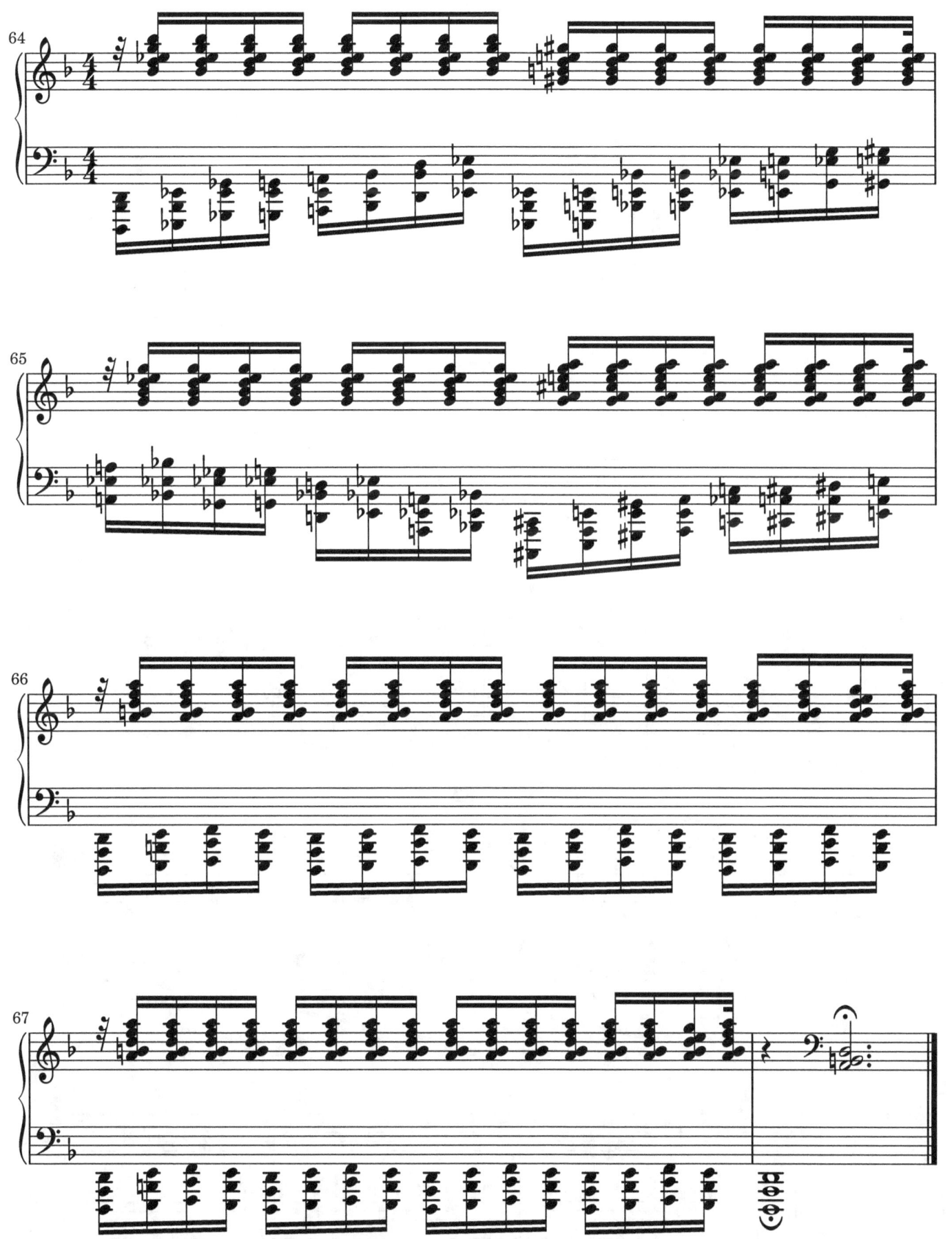

[*Construção*, Chico Buarque]

Pós-Tudo 4

para Paulo Álvares

Bruno Ruviaro

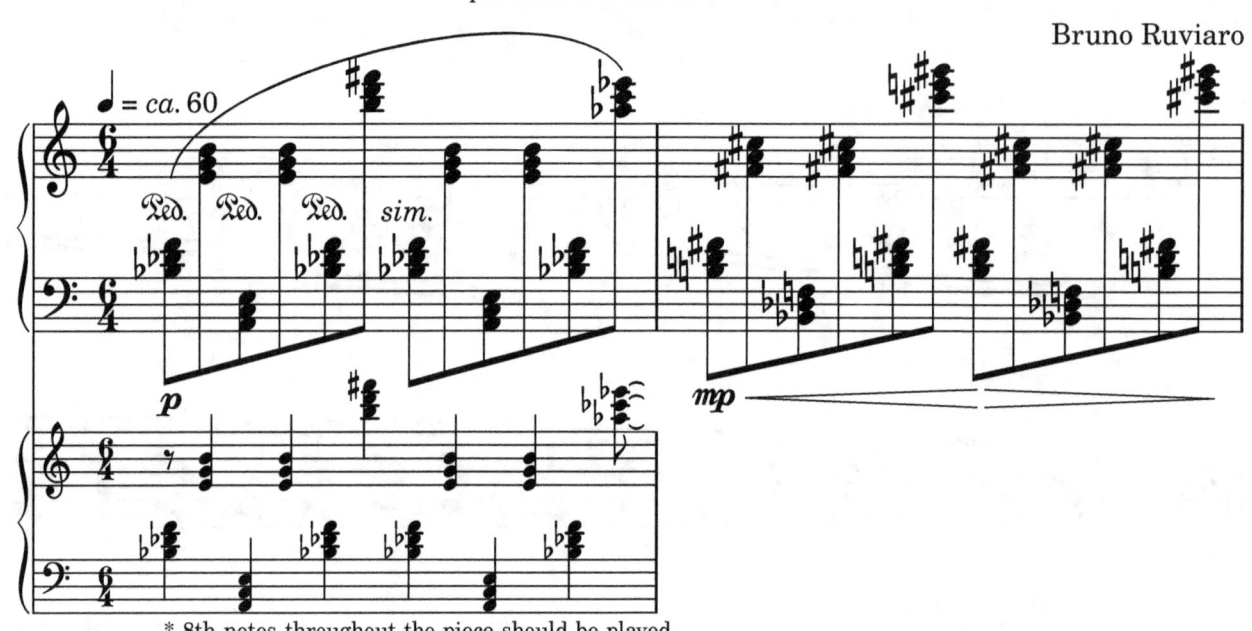

* 8th notes throughout the piece should be played
molto legato, almost as overlapping quarter notes.
* Accidentals apply only to one note.

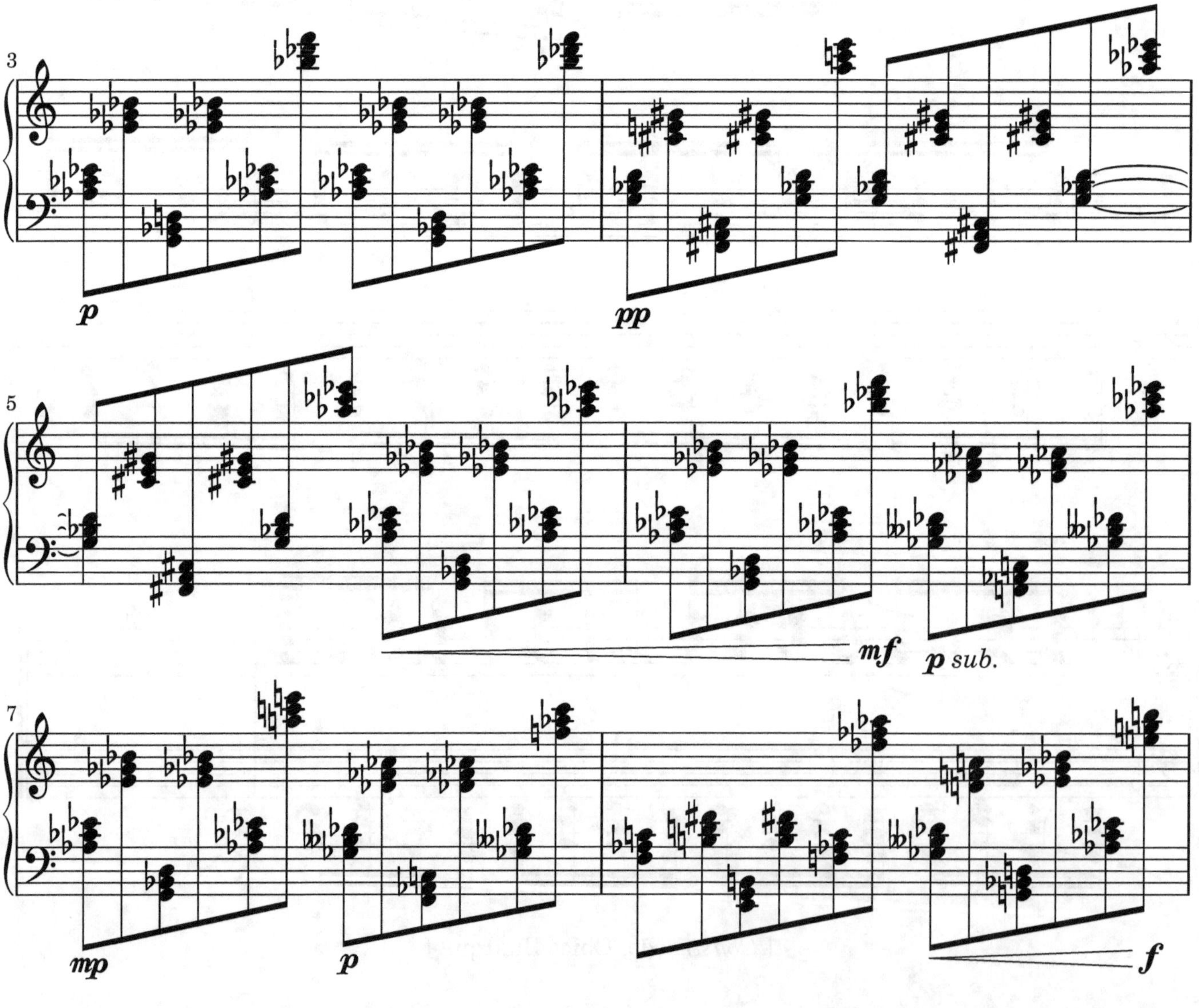

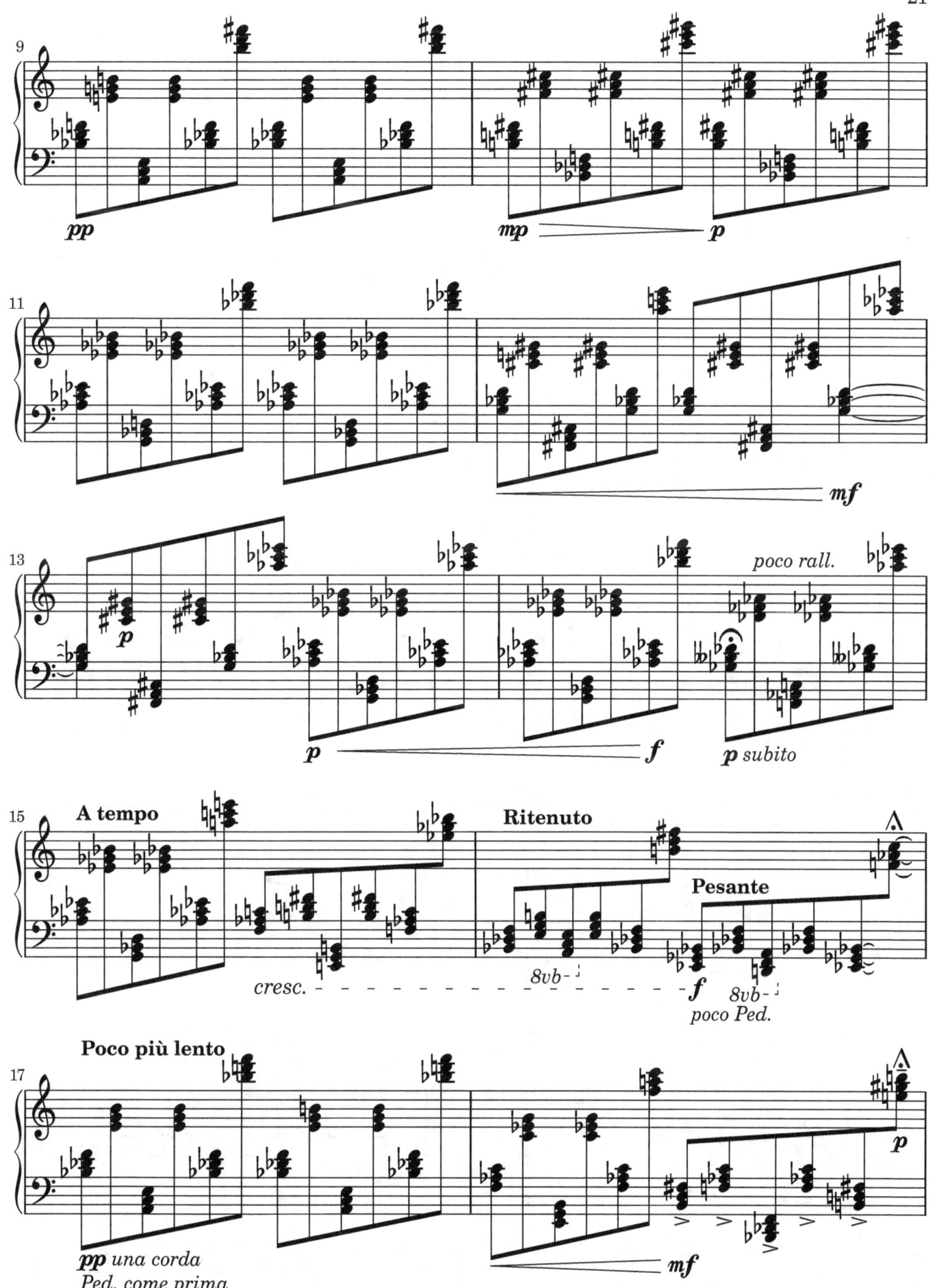

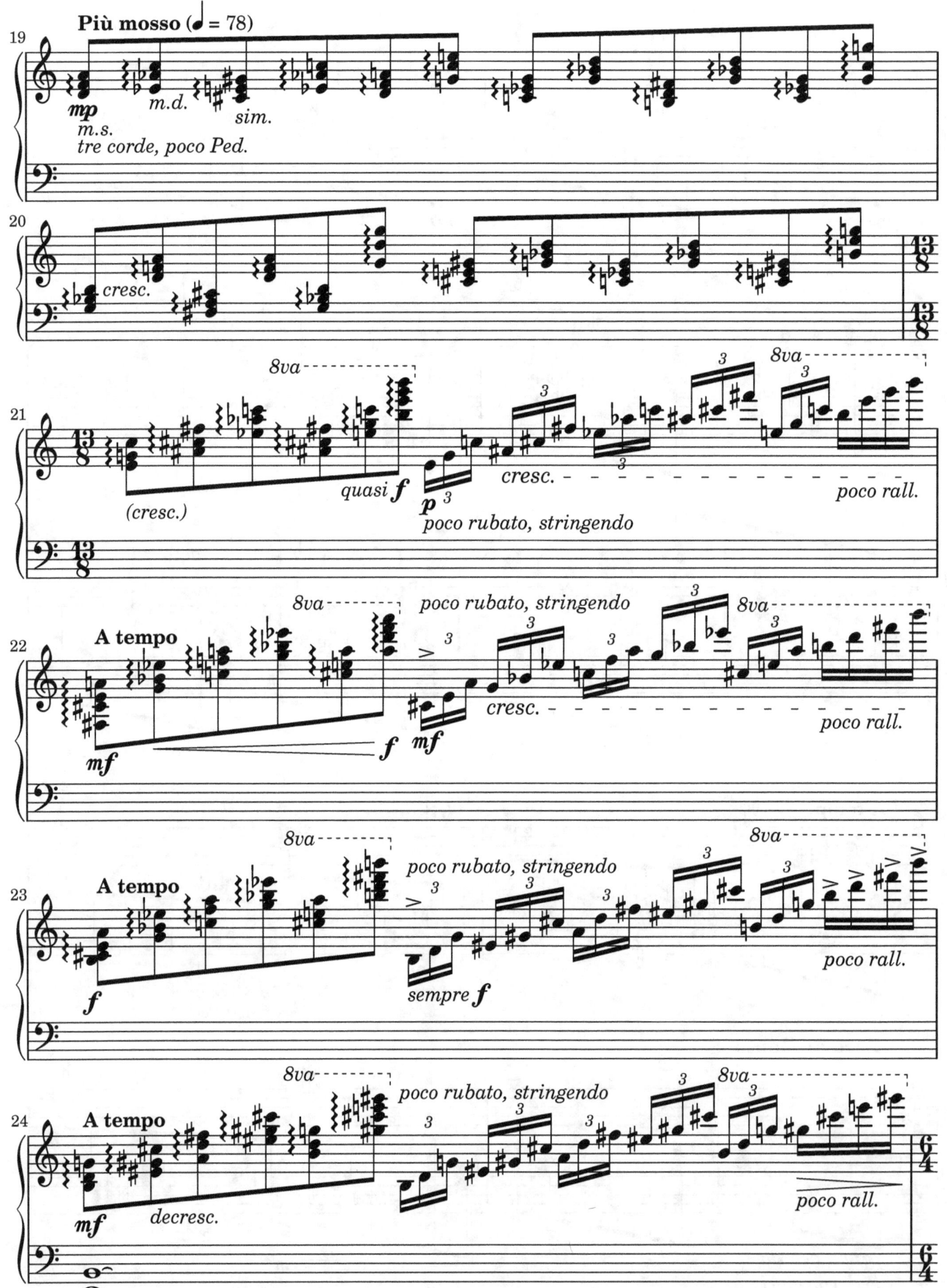

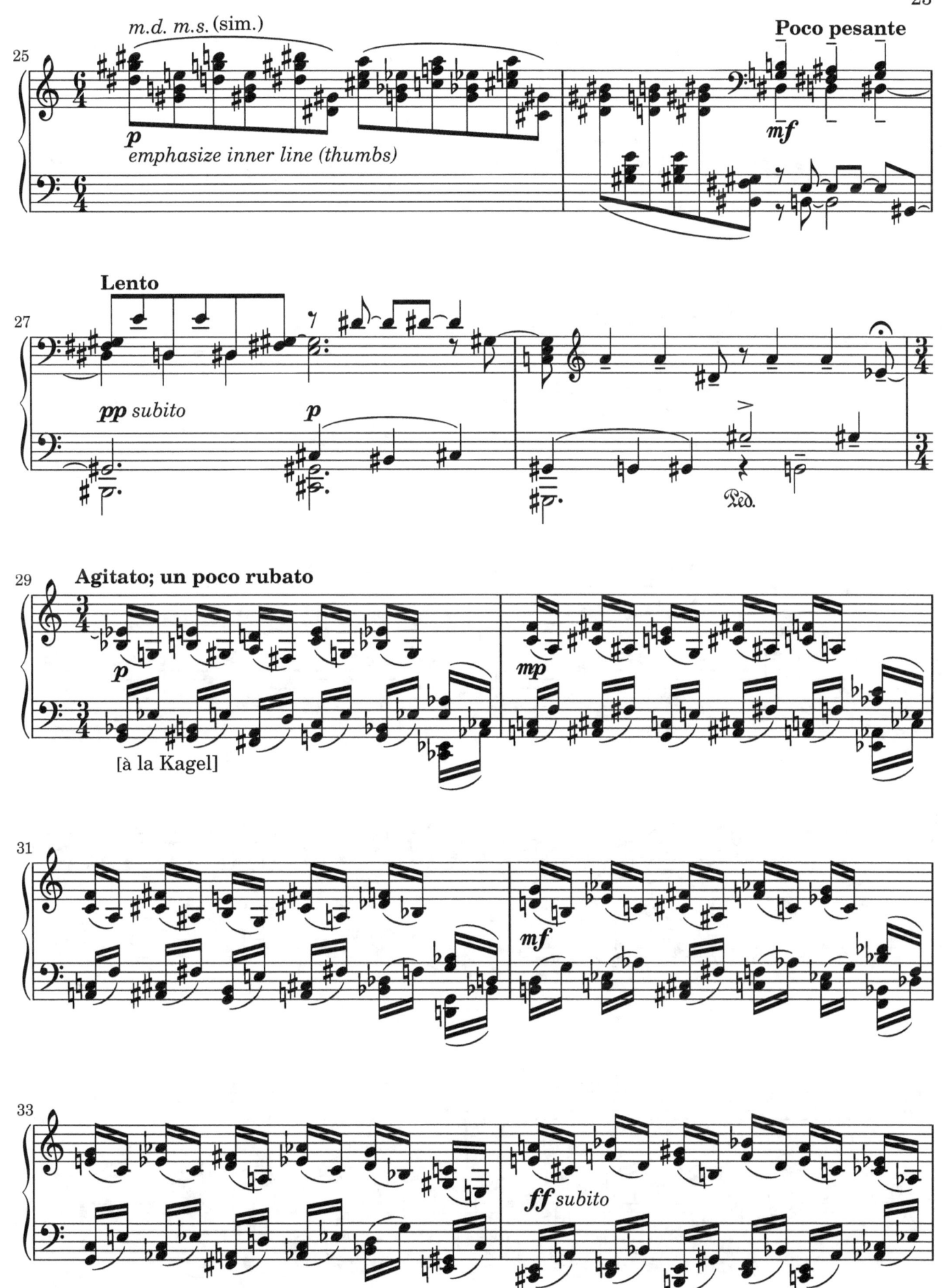

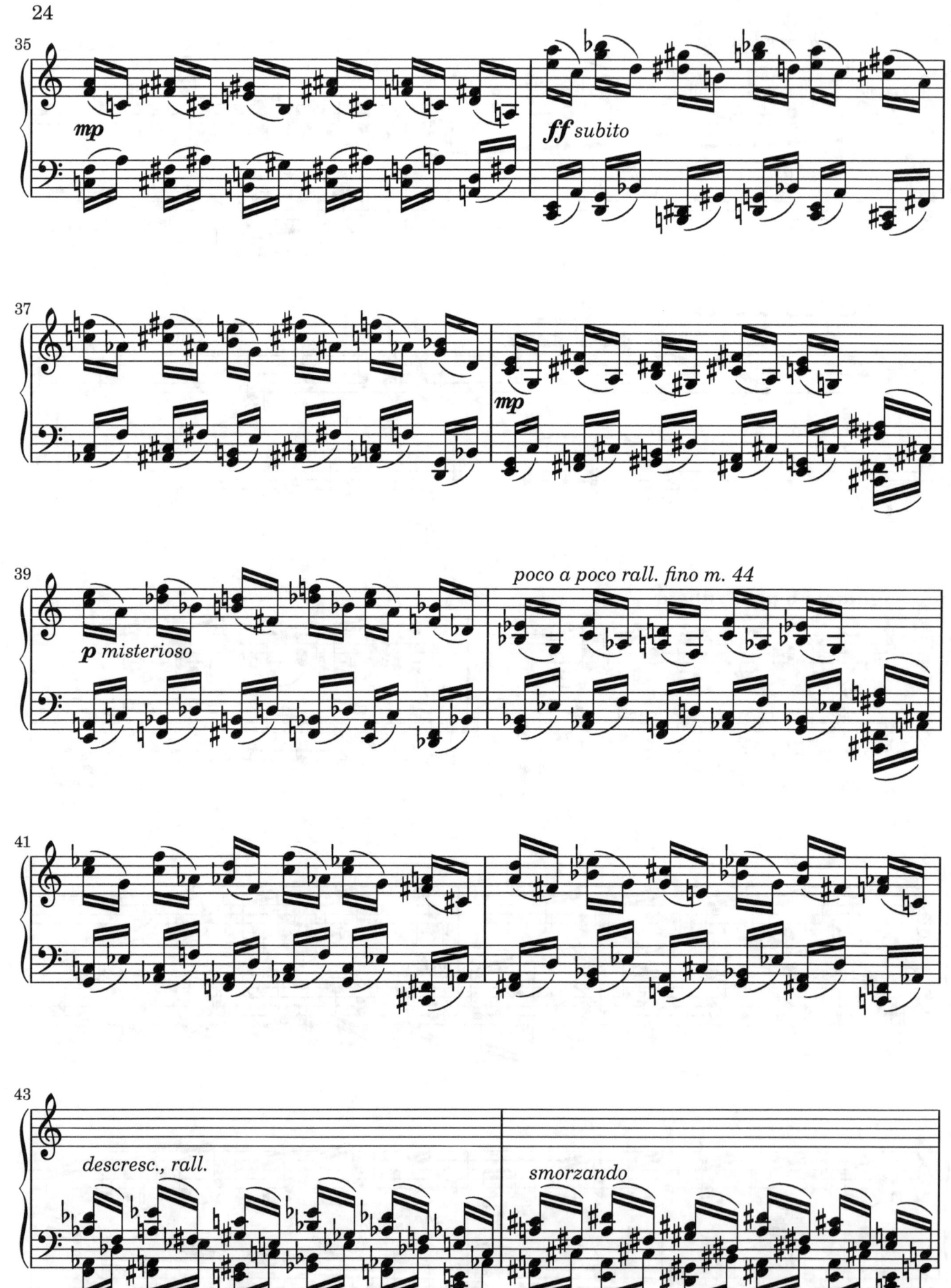

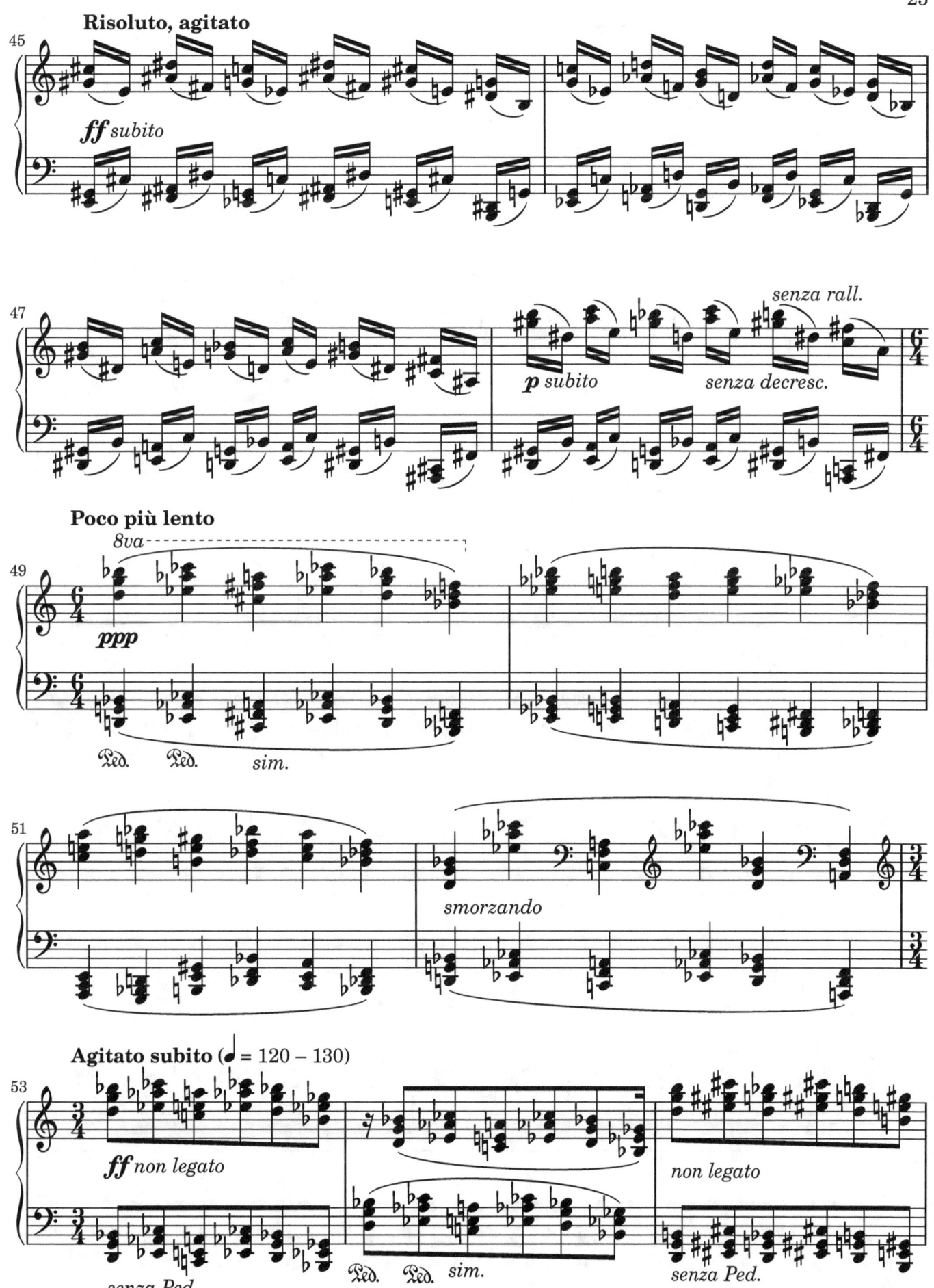

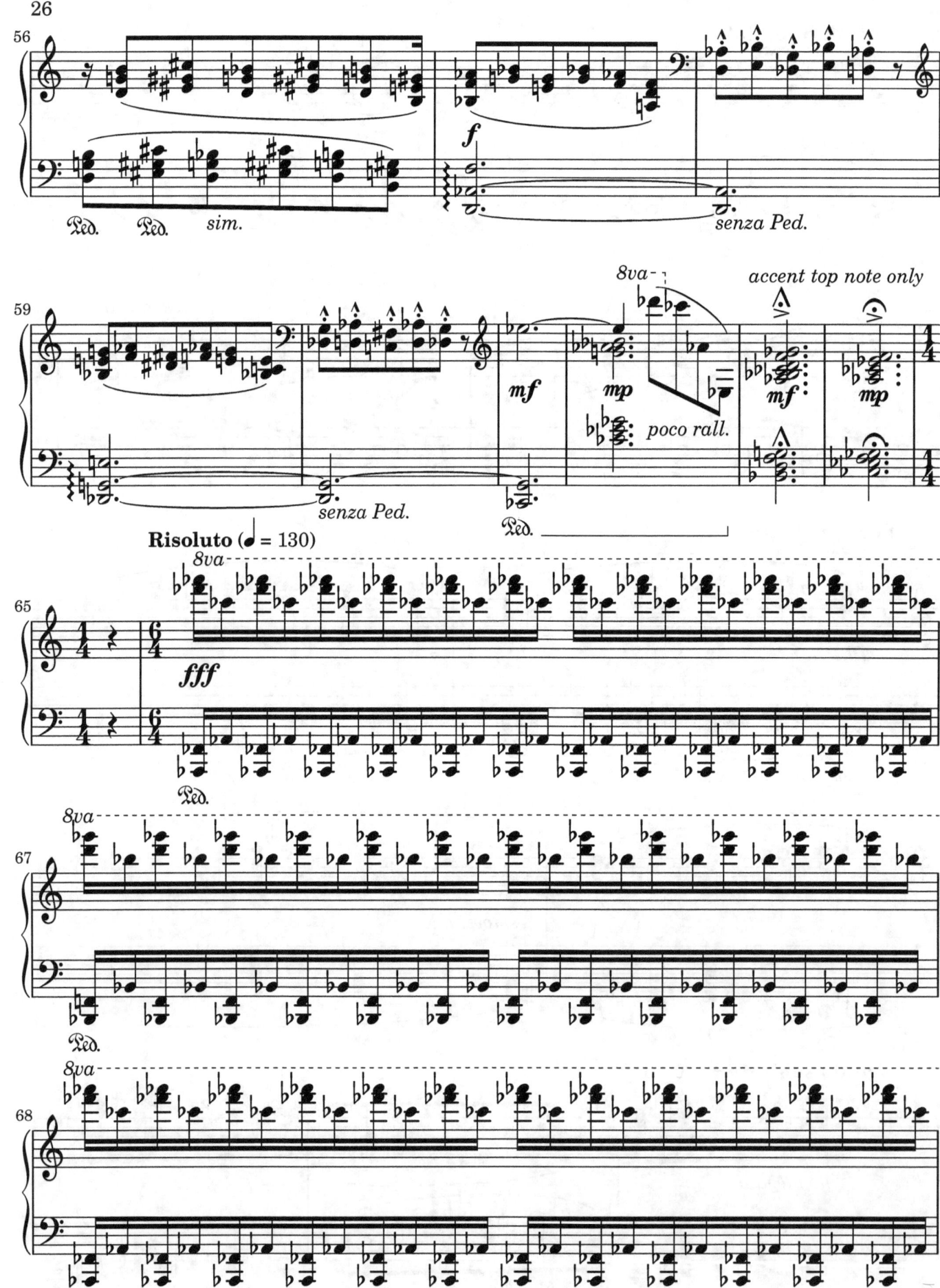

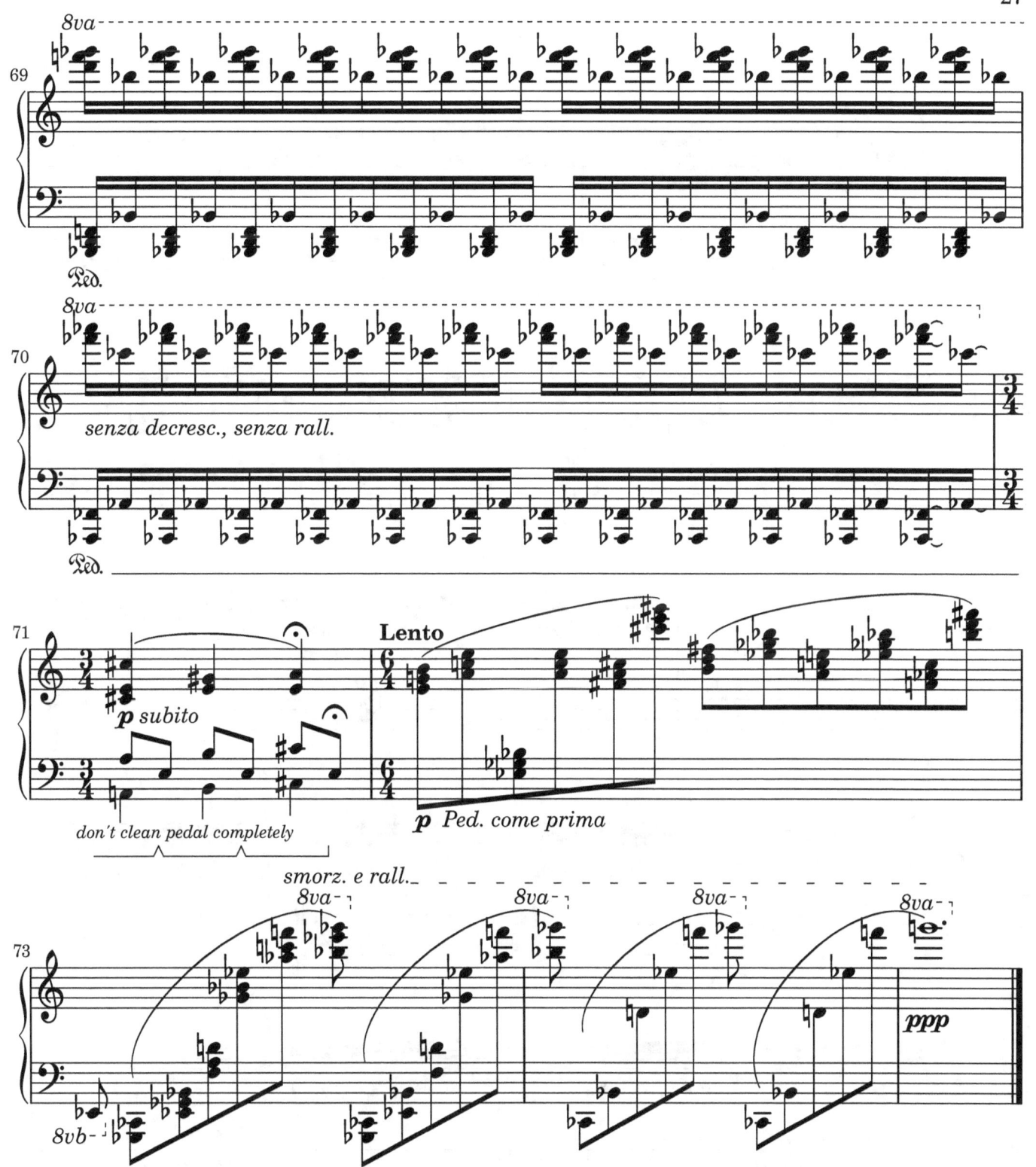

[*Étude Op. 10 #6, Chopin*]

Pós-Tudo 5

Bruno Ruviaro

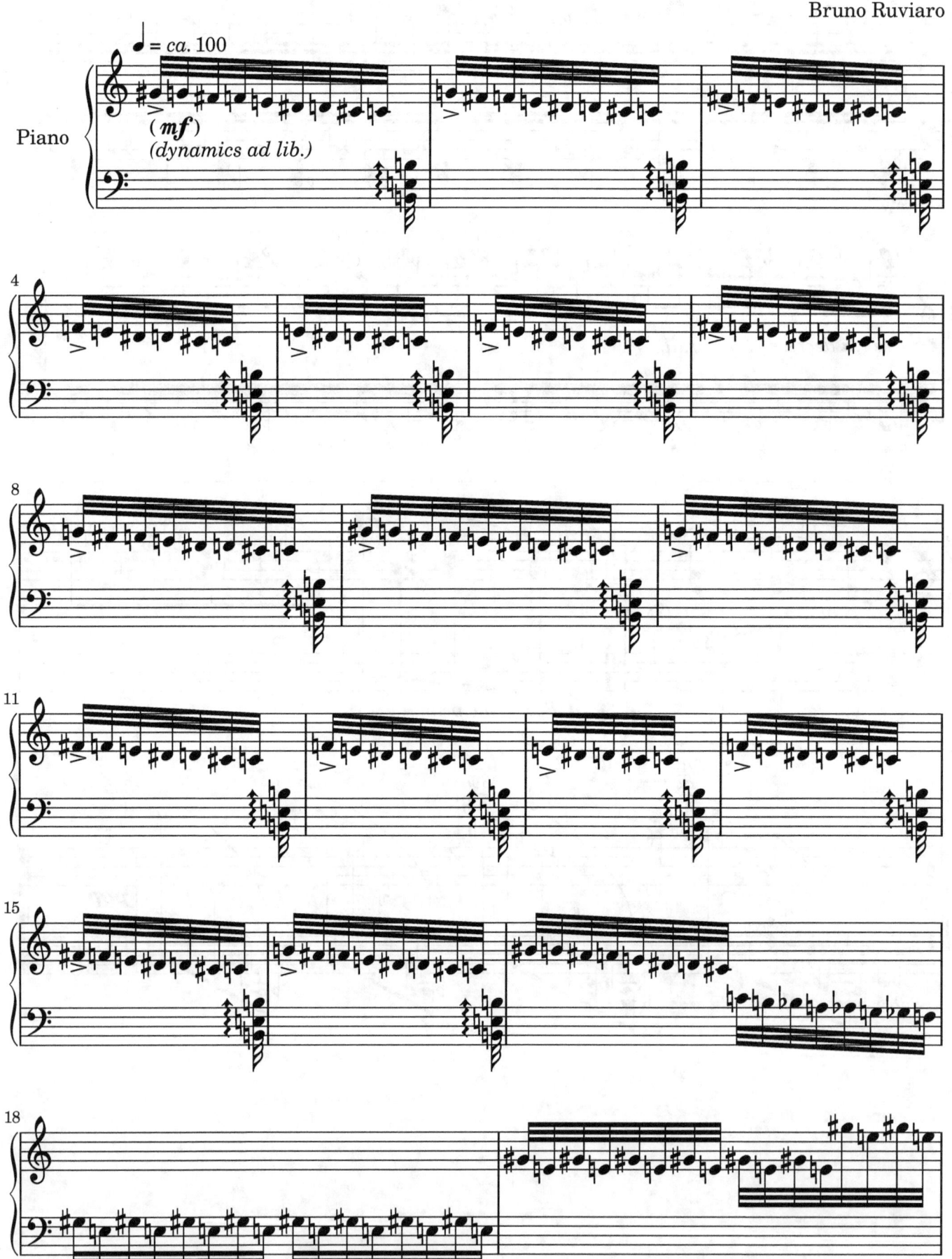

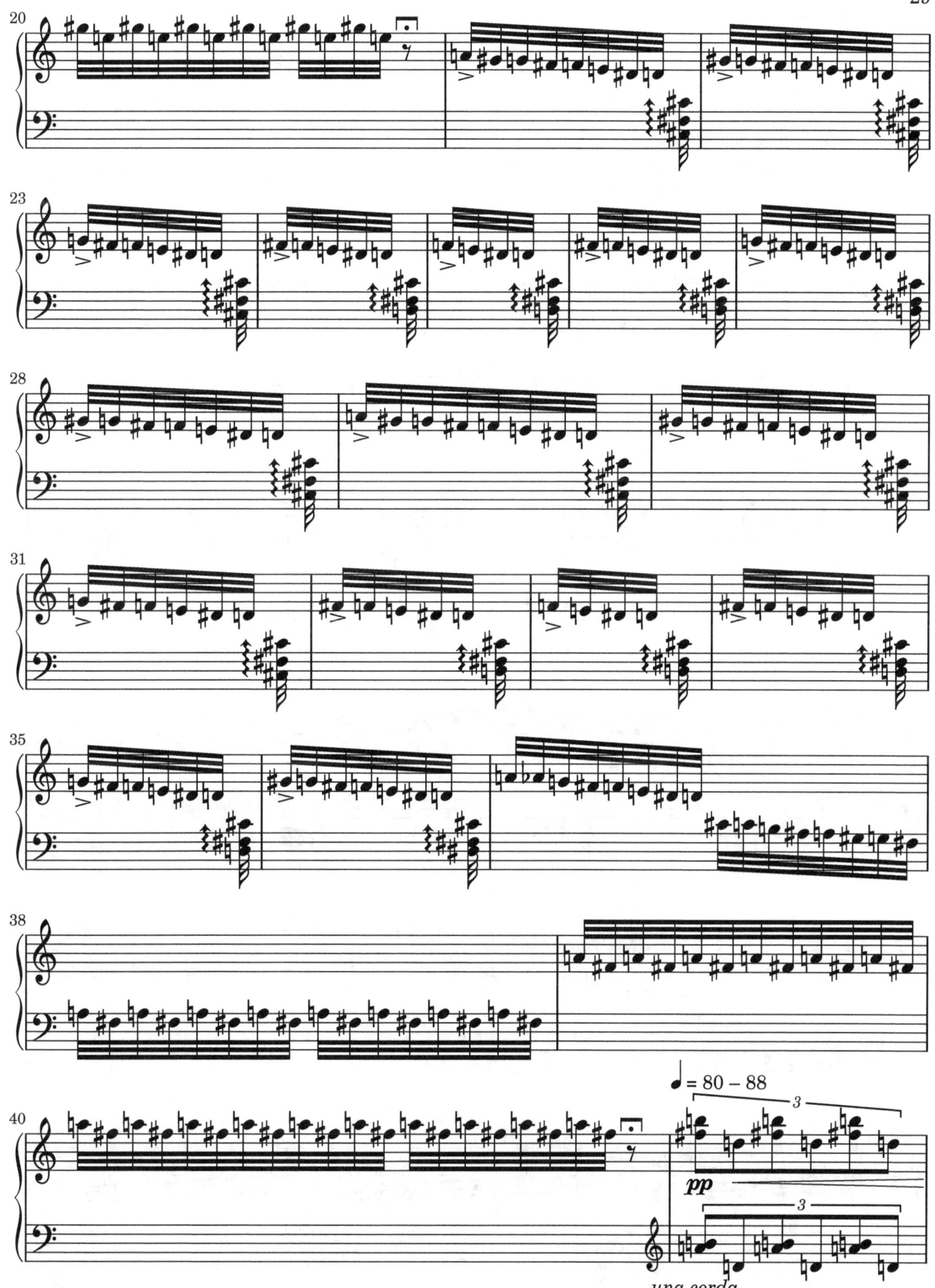

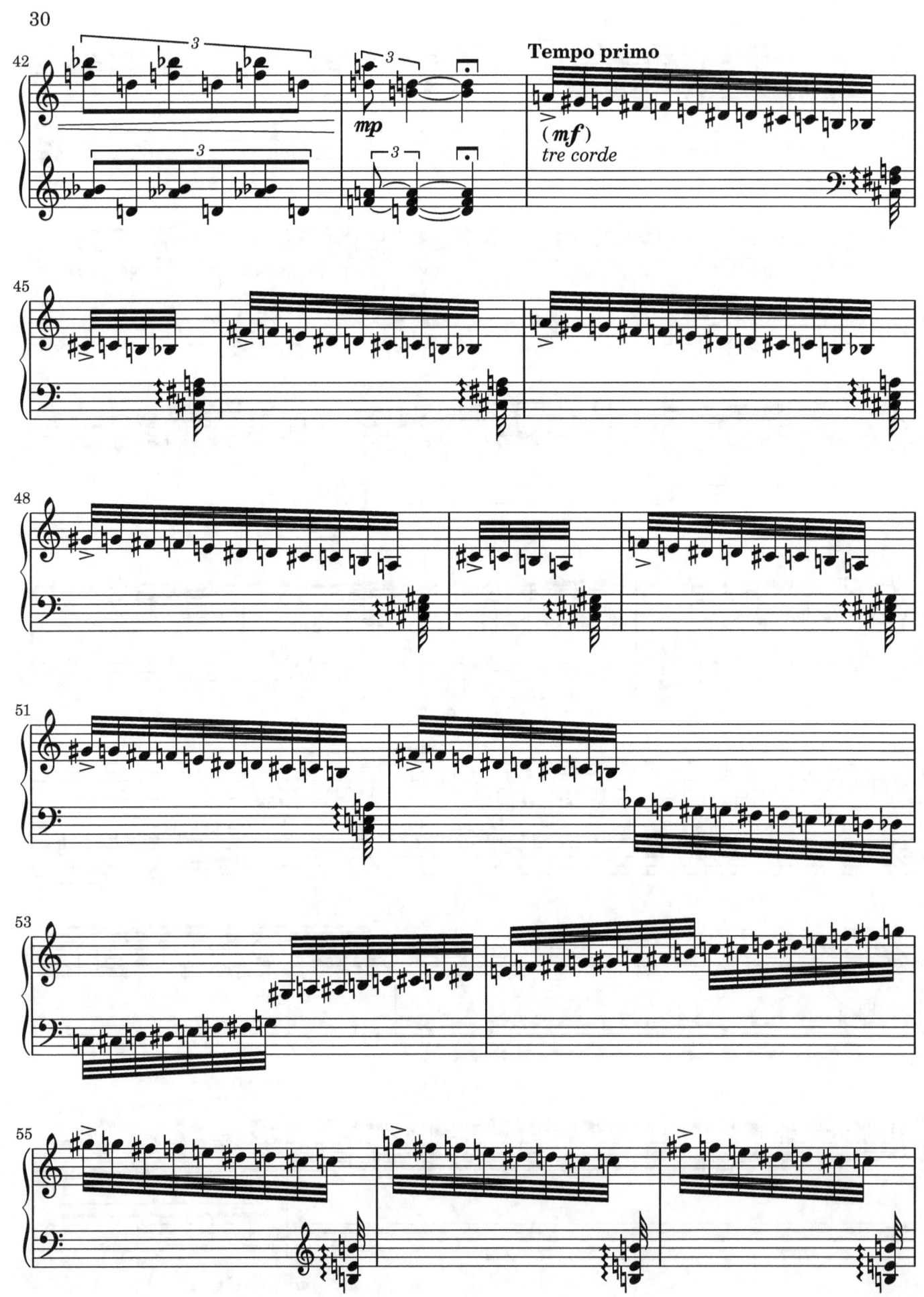

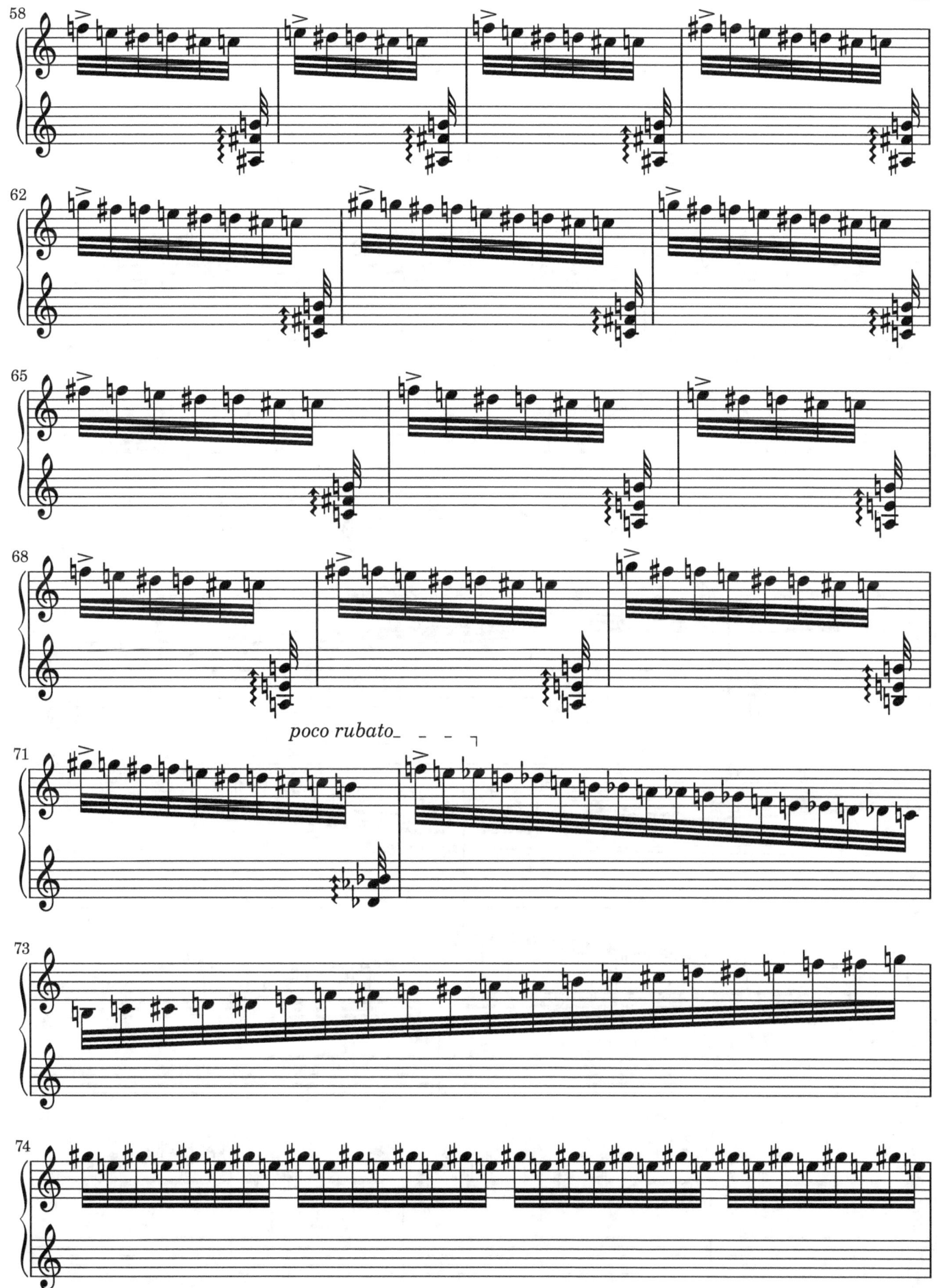

poco rubato

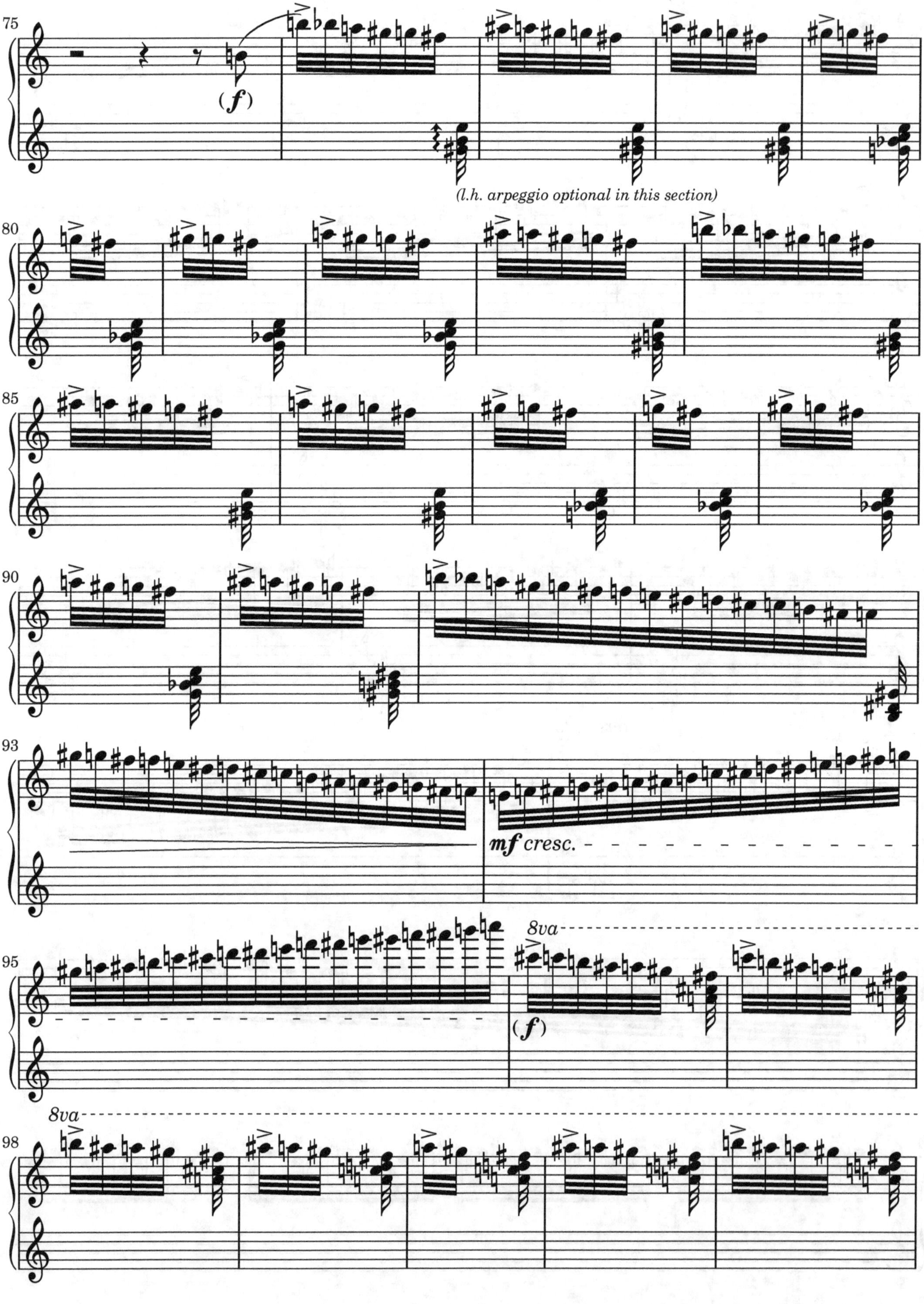

(l.h. arpeggio optional in this section)

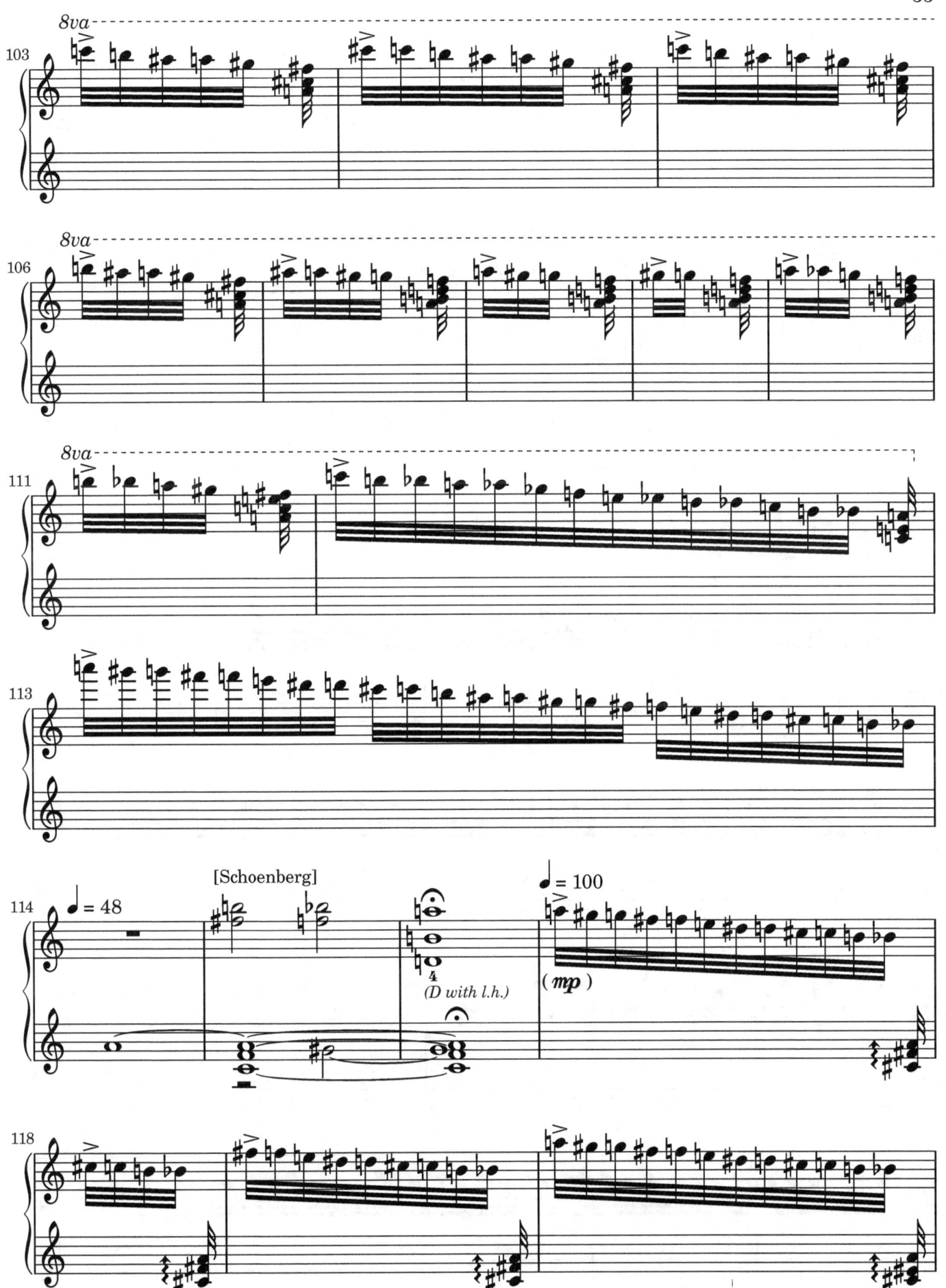

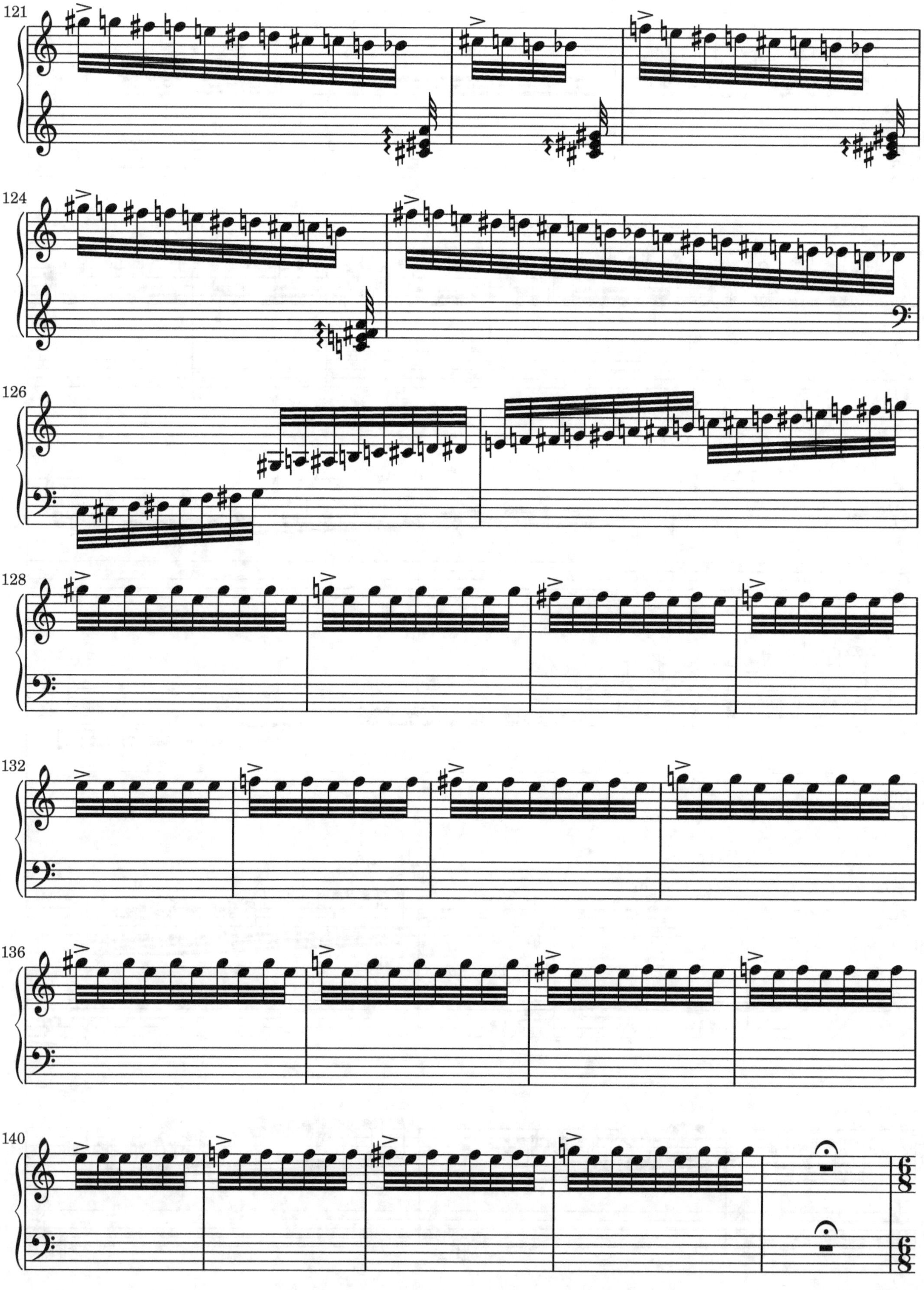

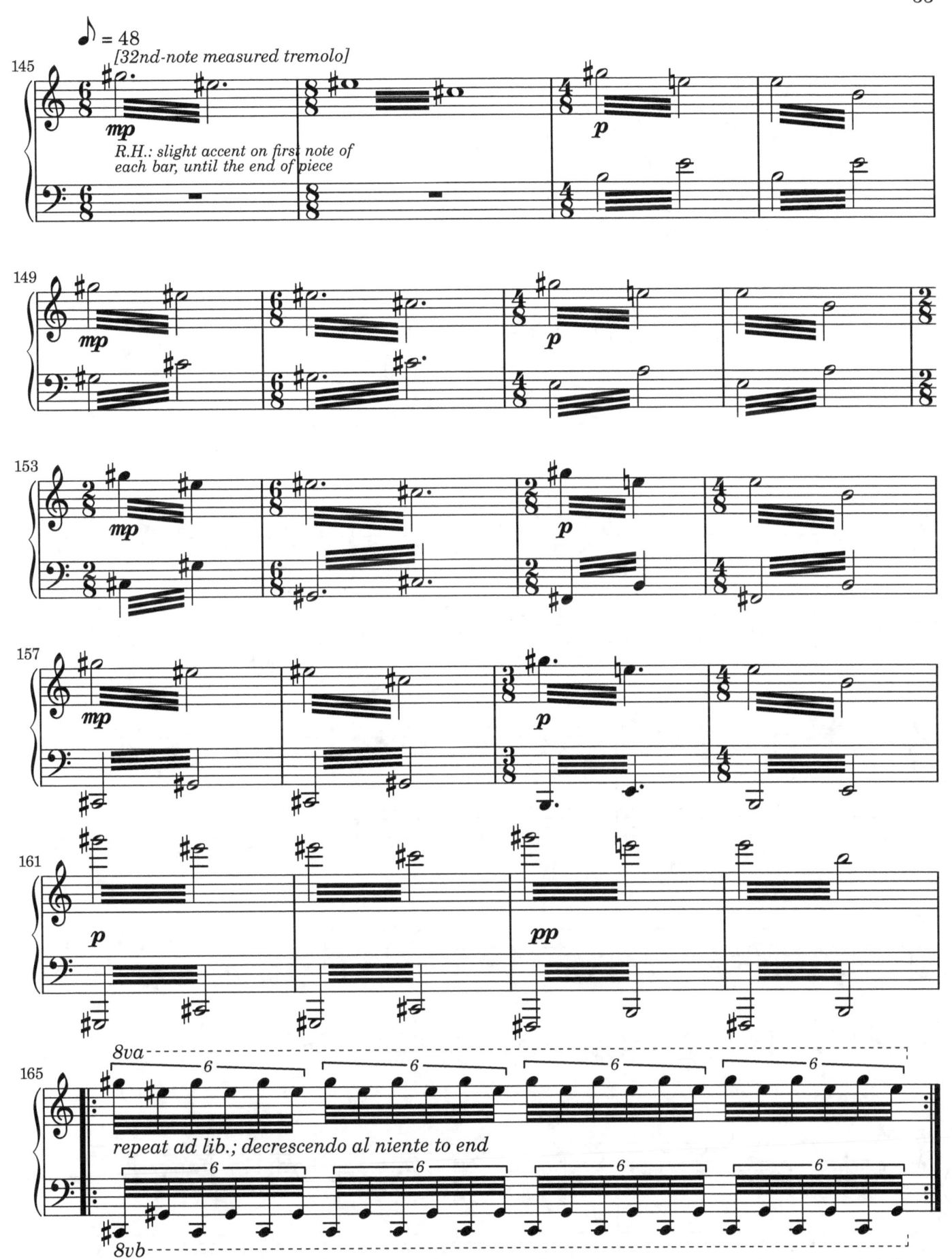

[*A Ostra e o Vento*, Chico Buarque]

Pós-Tudo 6

Bruno Ruviaro

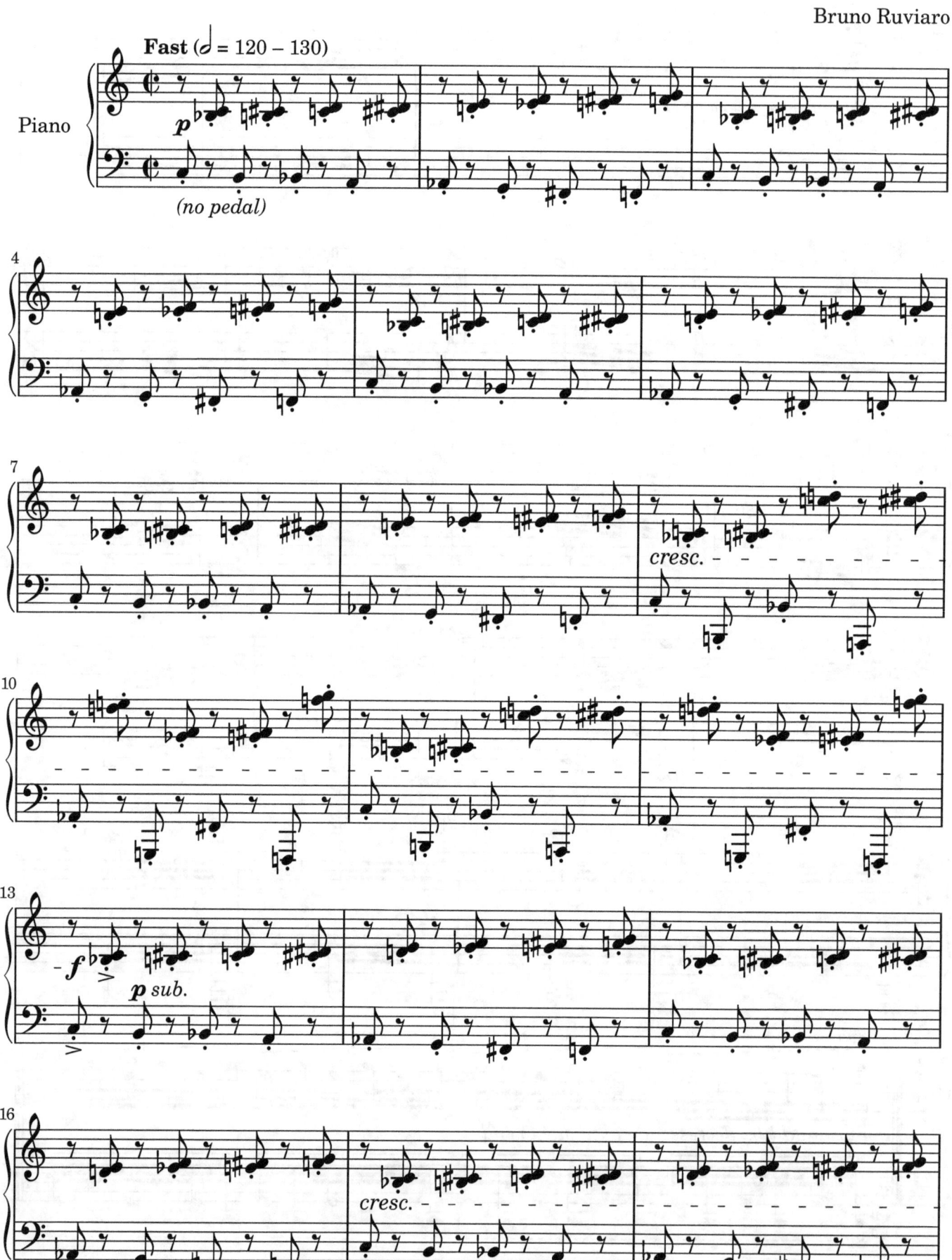

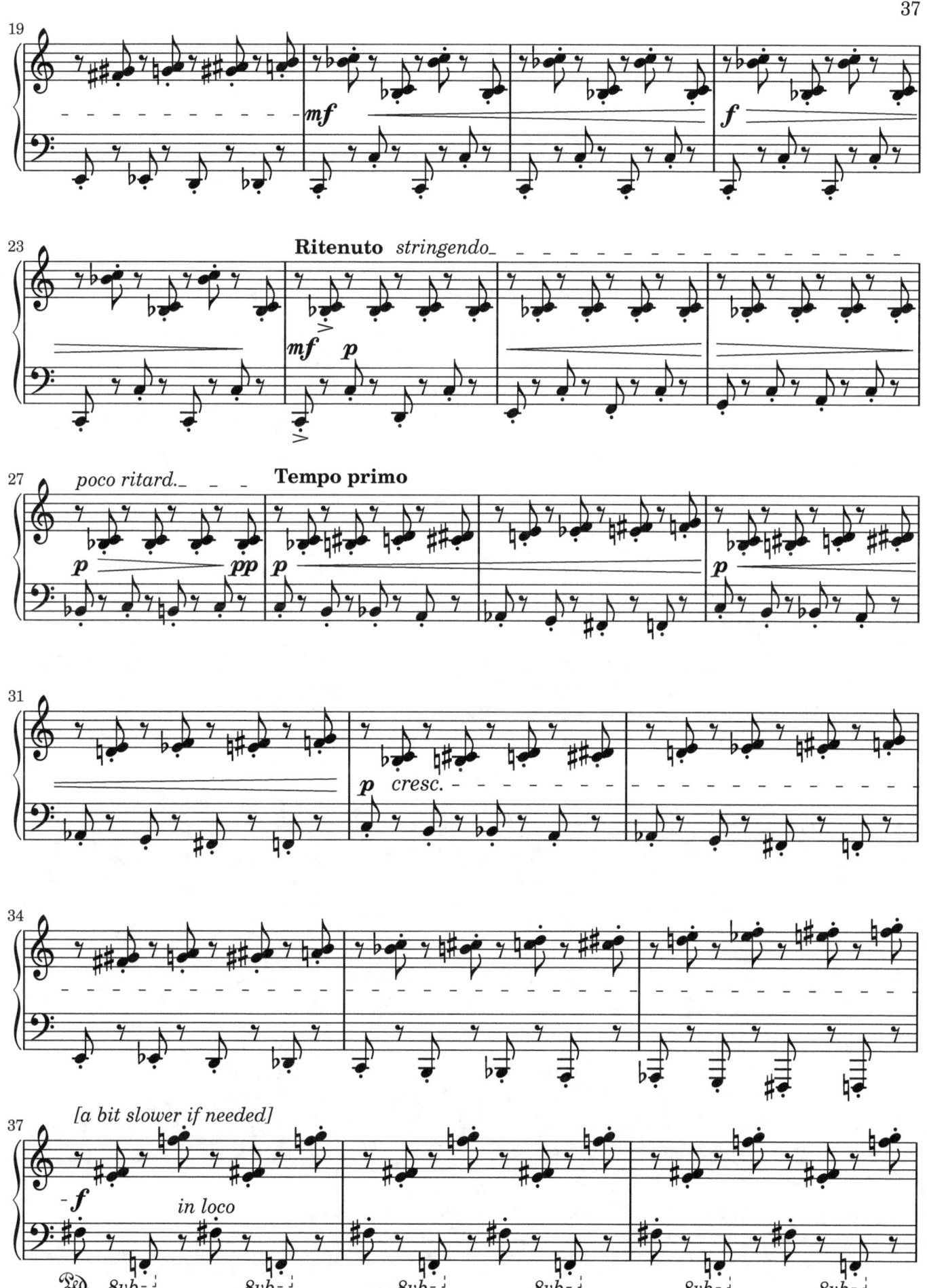

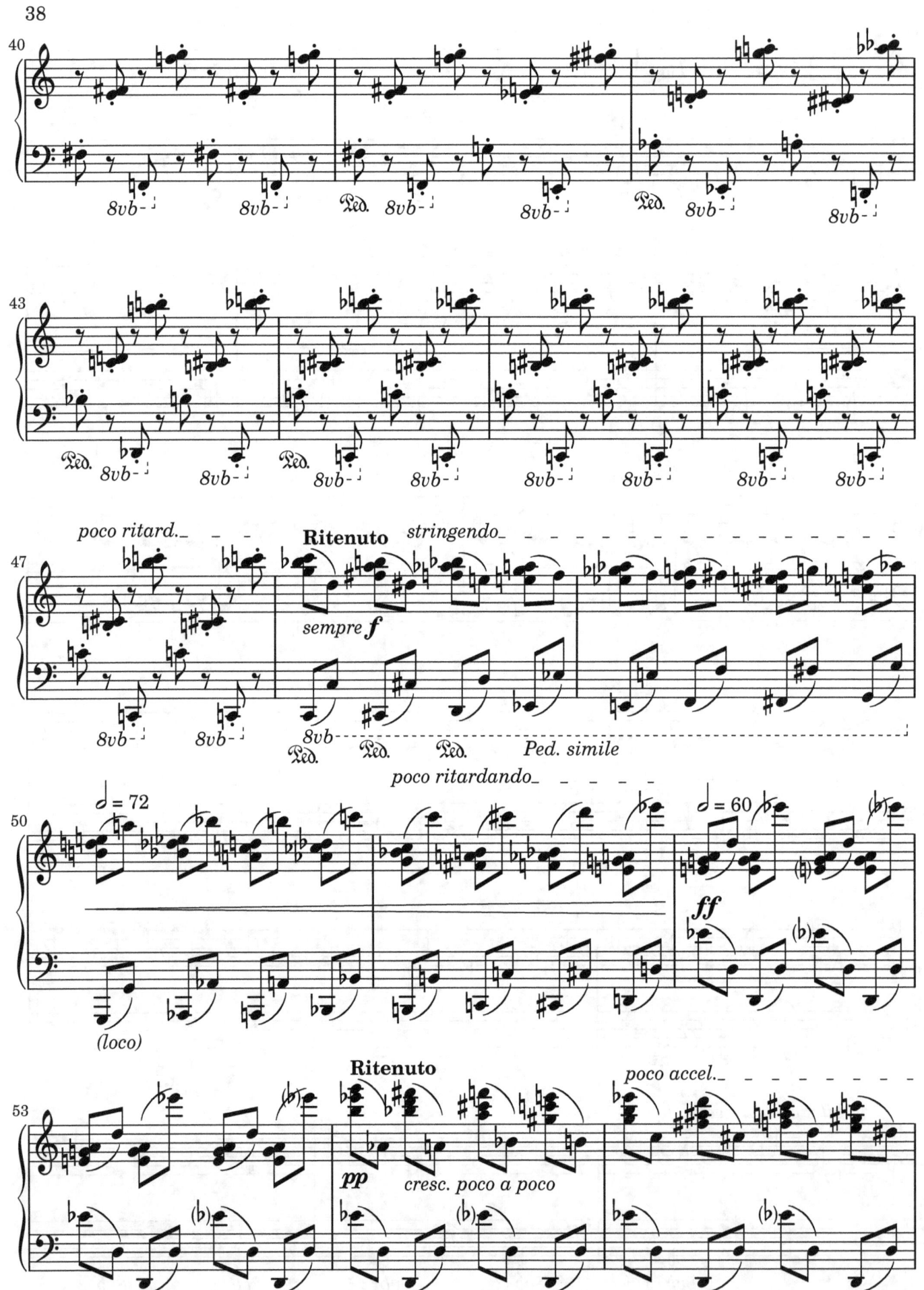

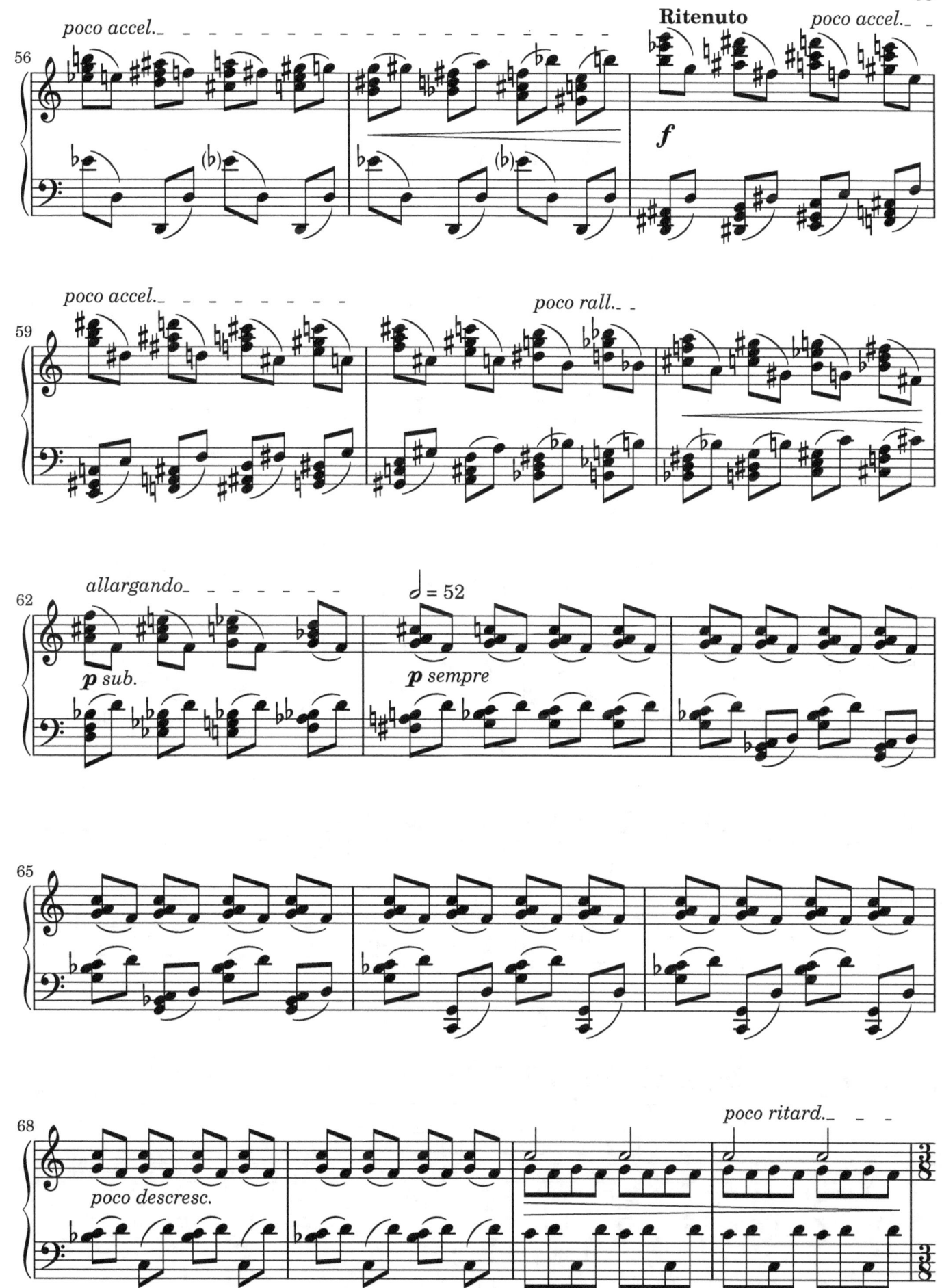

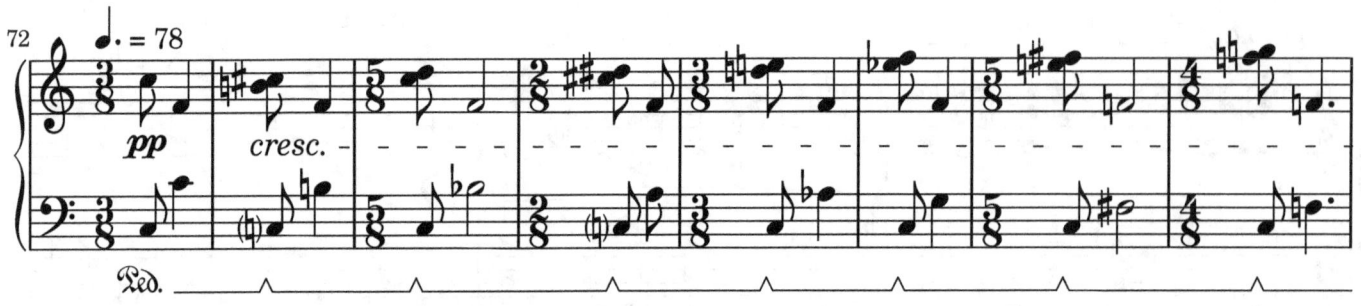

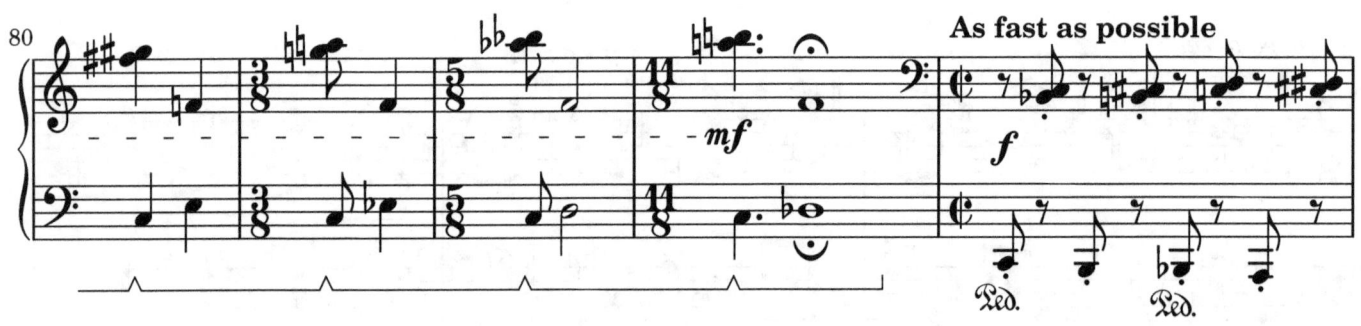

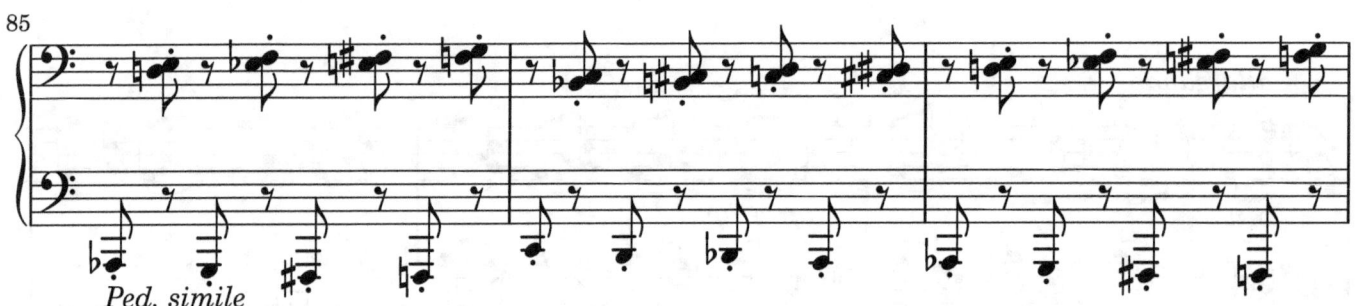

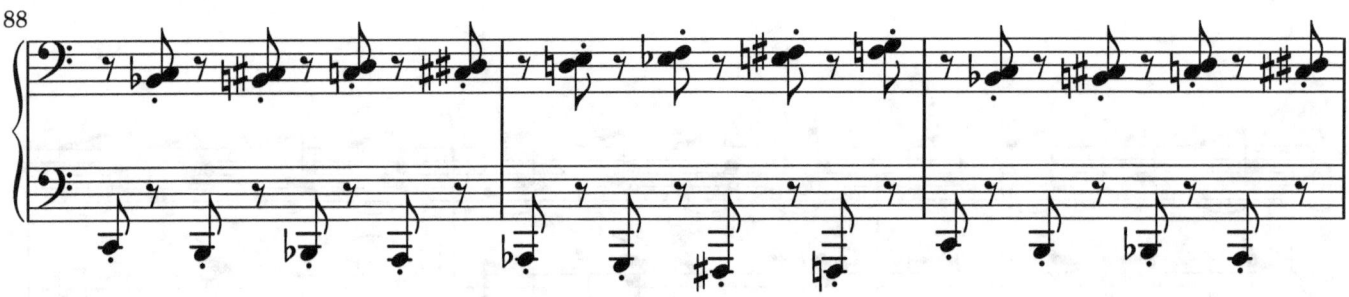

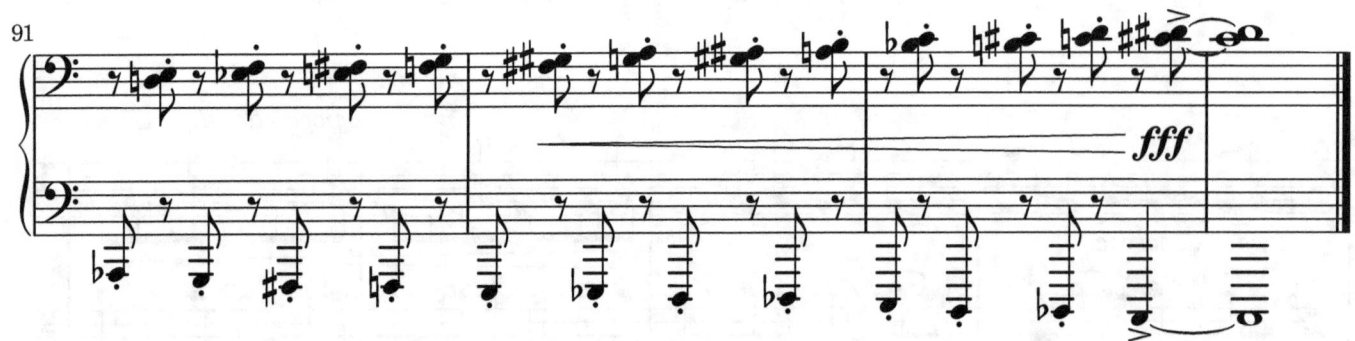

[ ]

Pós-Tudo 7

Bruno Ruviaro

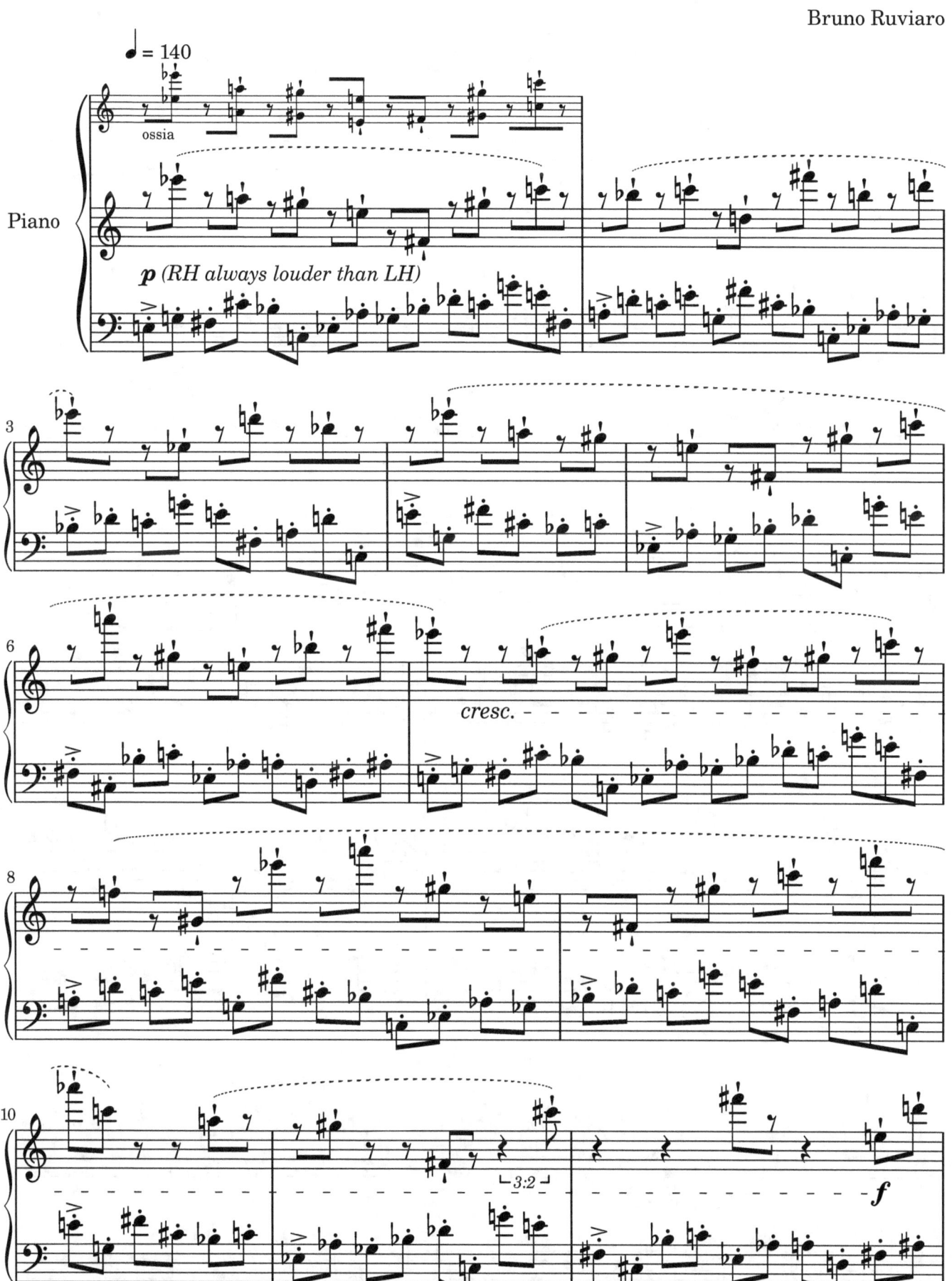

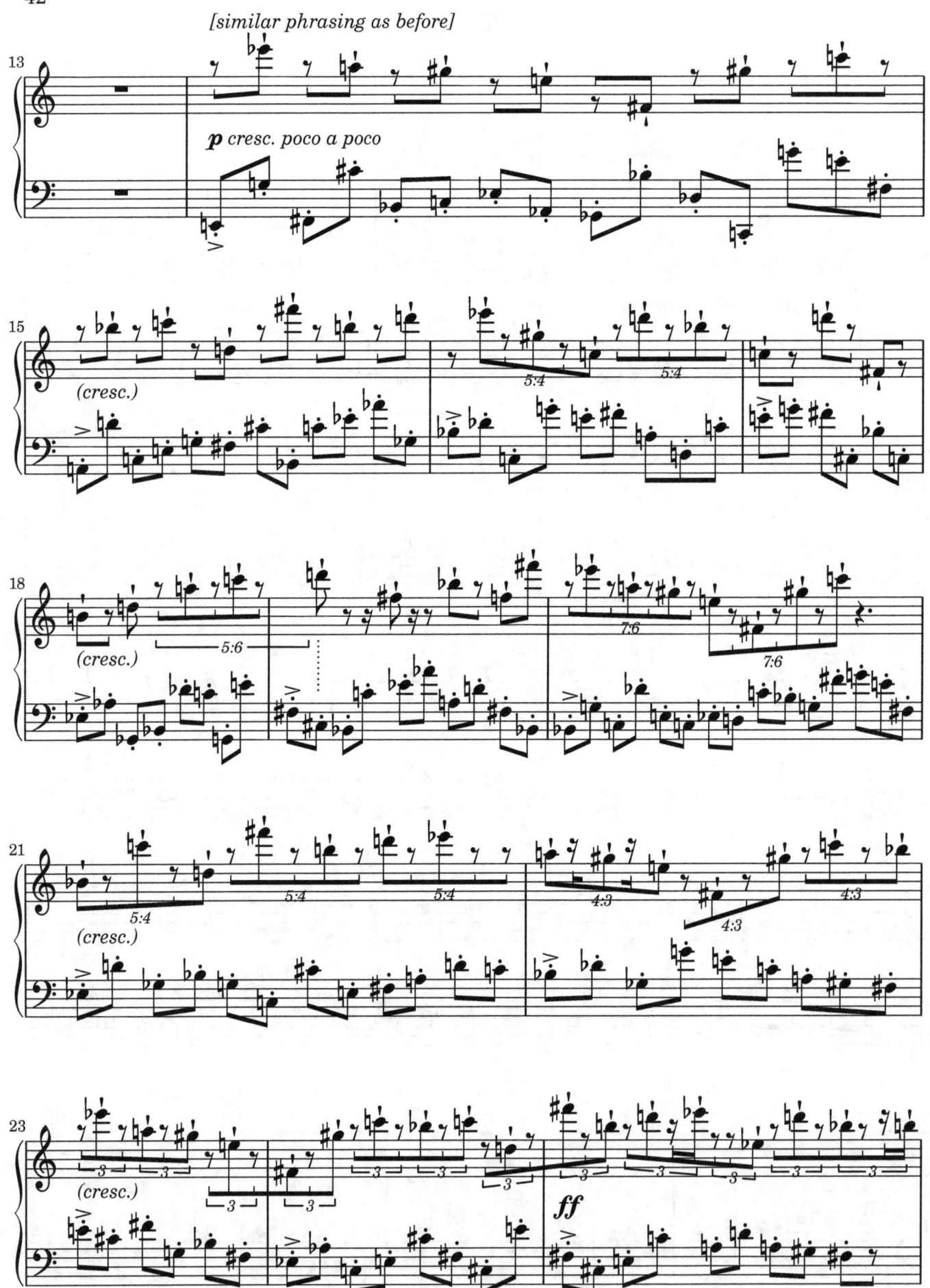

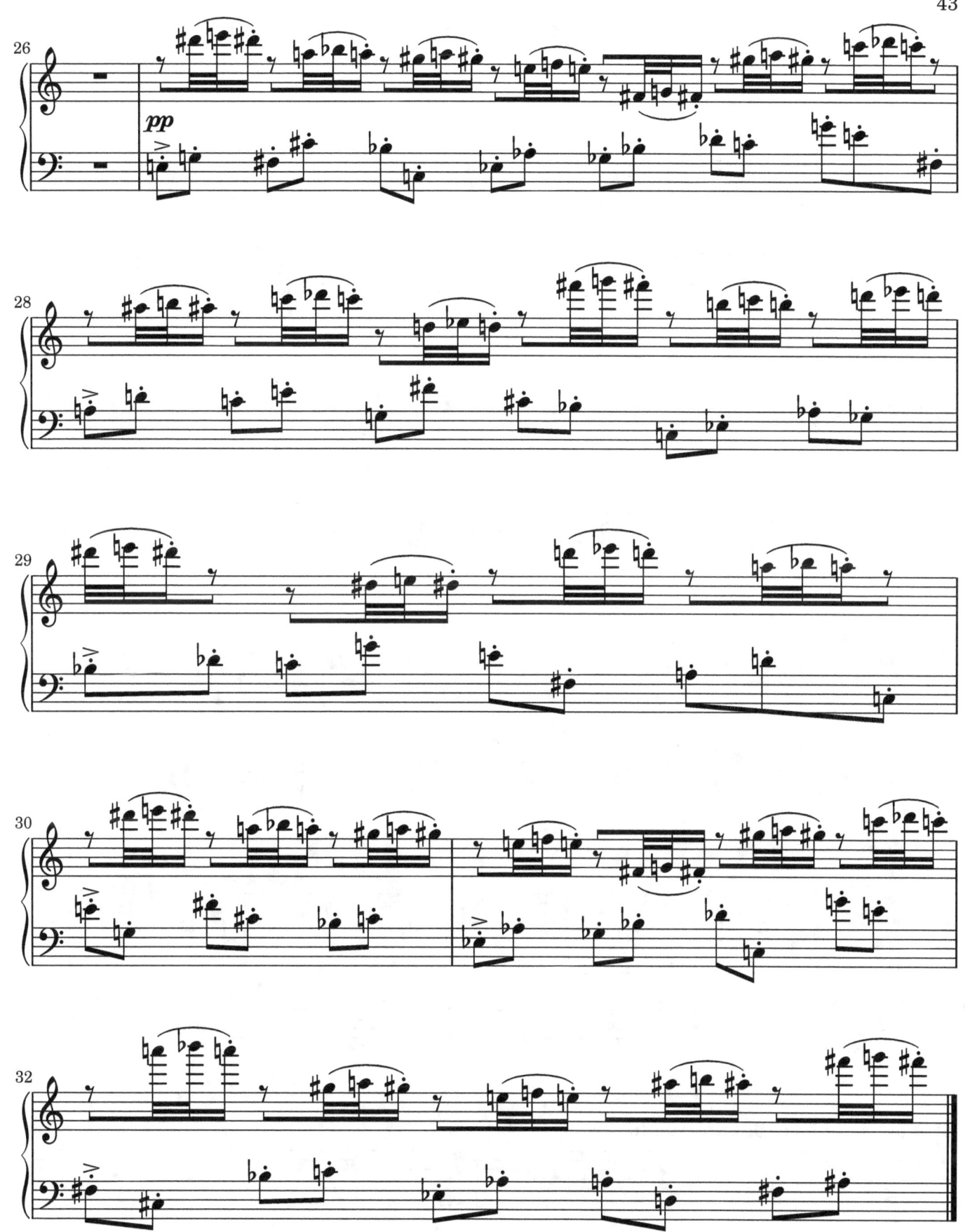

[*Seis Vícios de Garlândia, 3rd mov.*, Bruno Ruviaro]

Pós-Tudo 8

Bruno Ruviaro

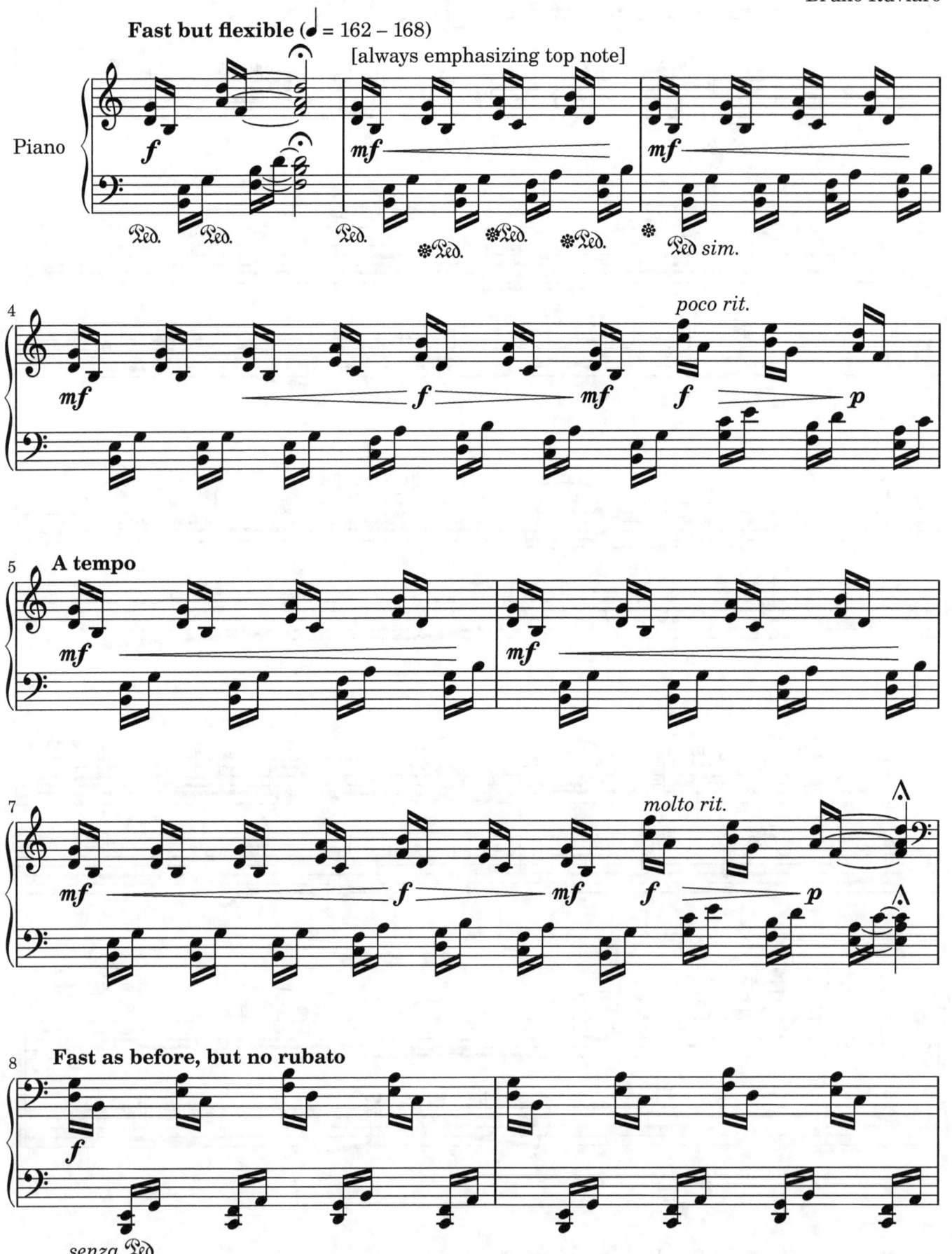

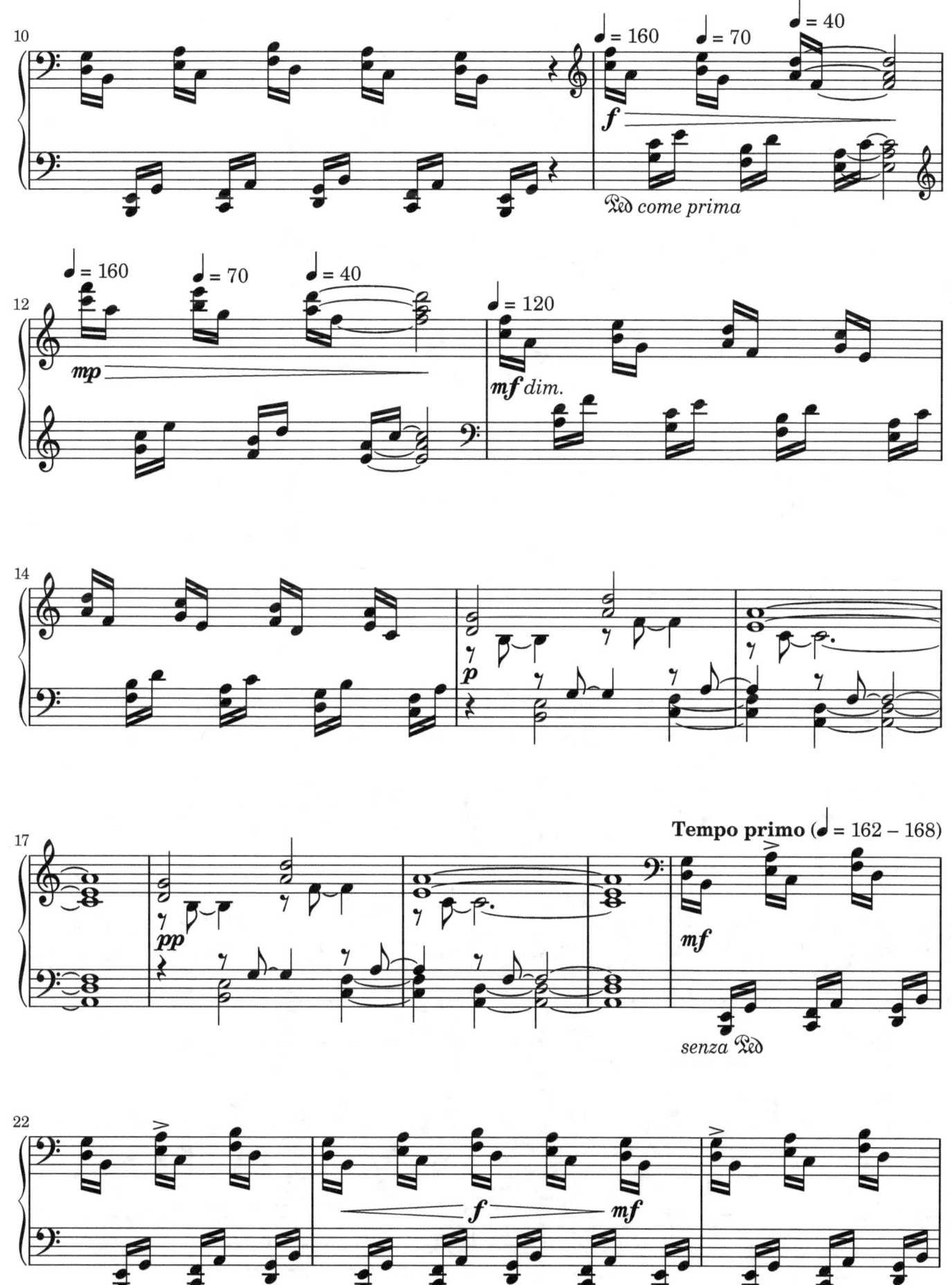

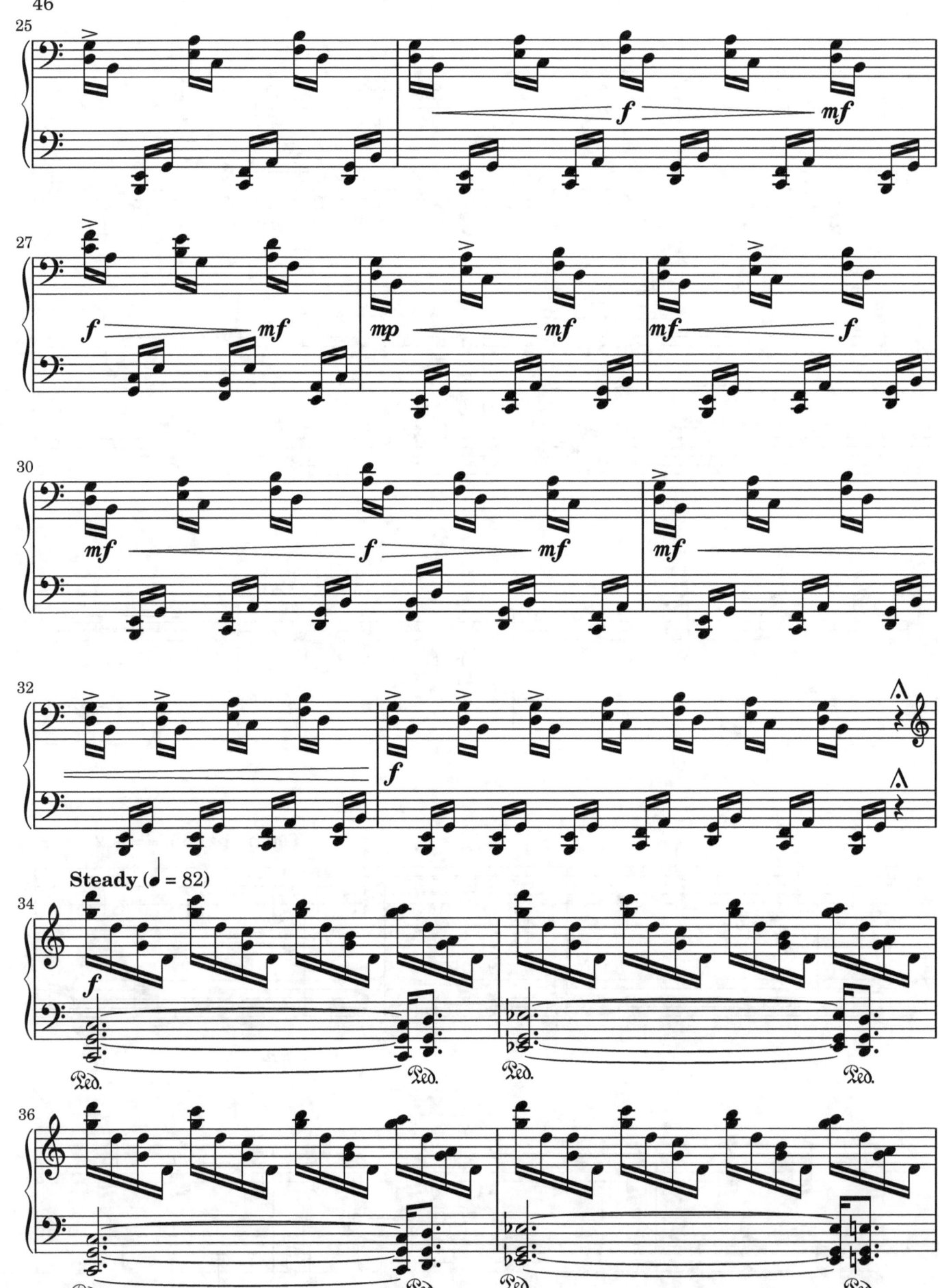

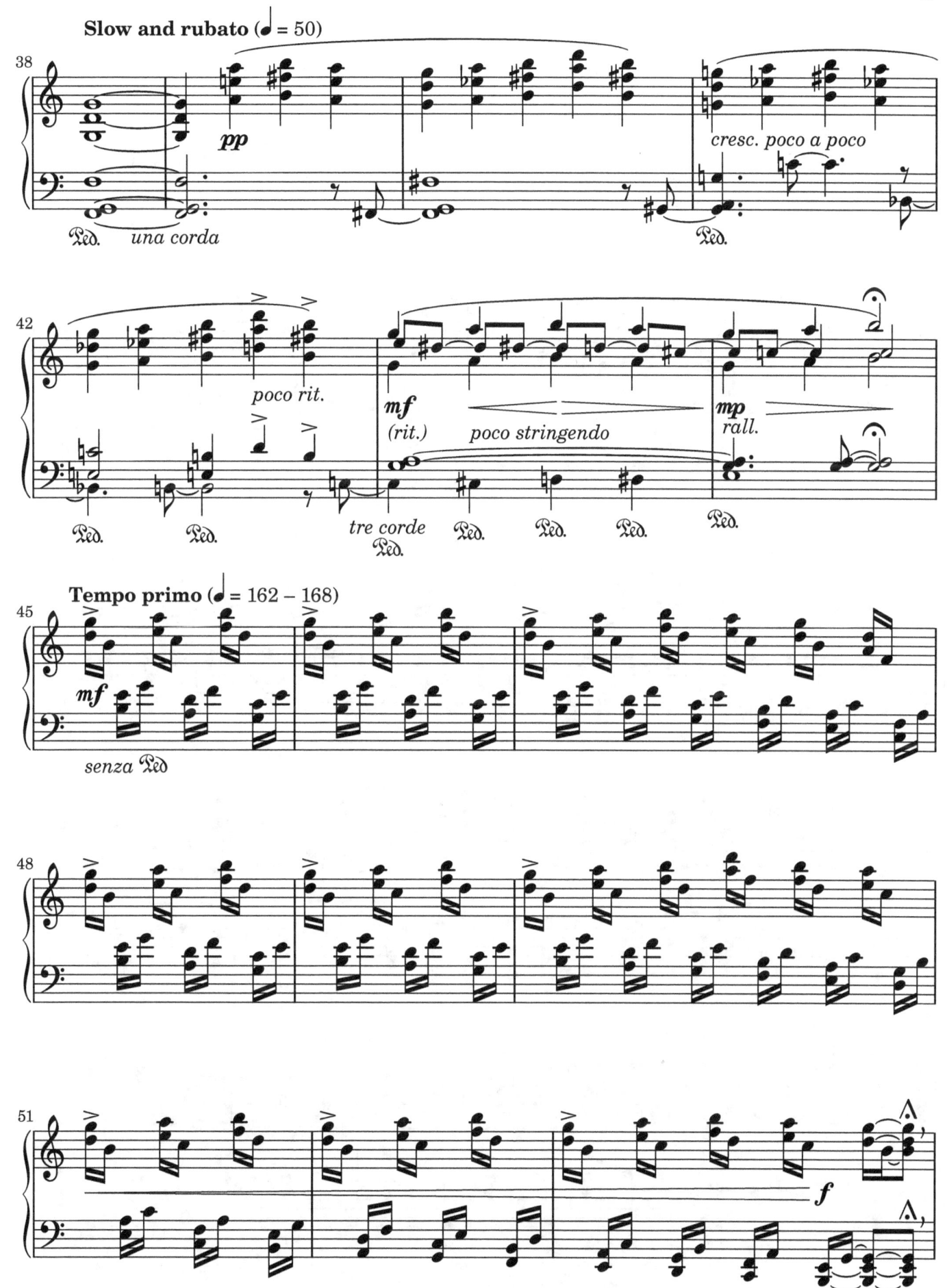

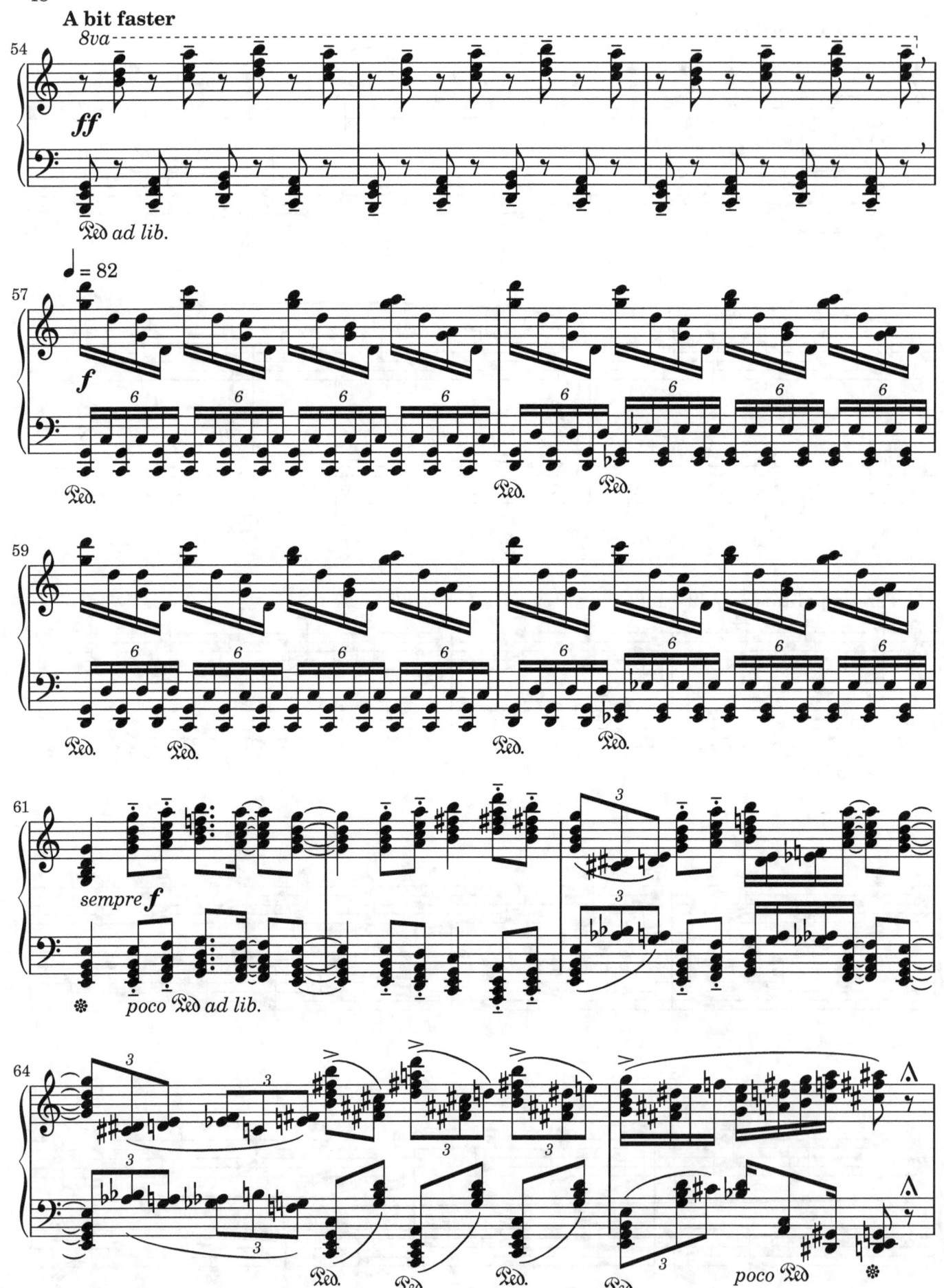

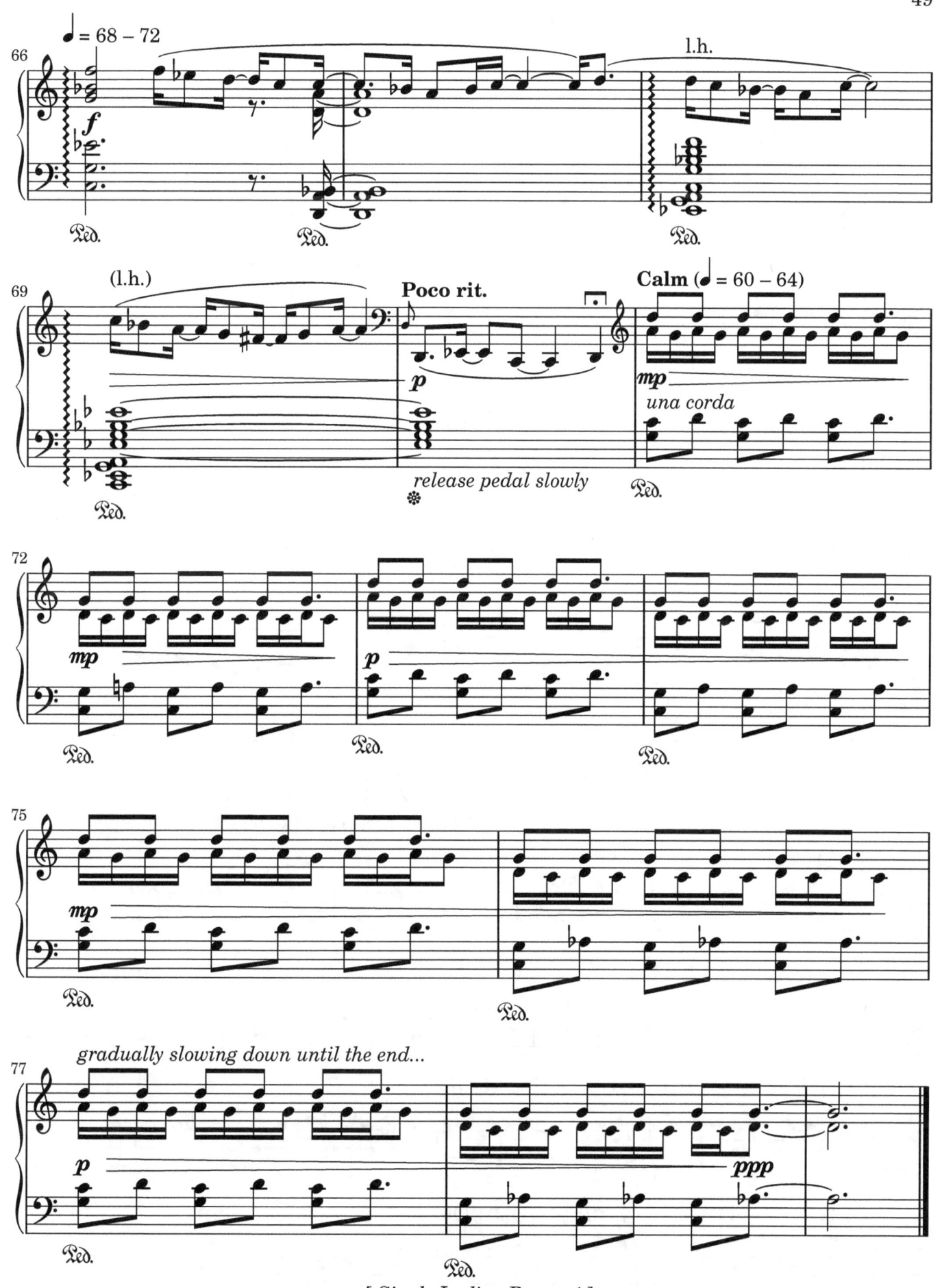

[*Single Ladies*, Beyoncé]

Pós-Tudo 9

for Kyle Adam Blair

Bruno Ruviaro

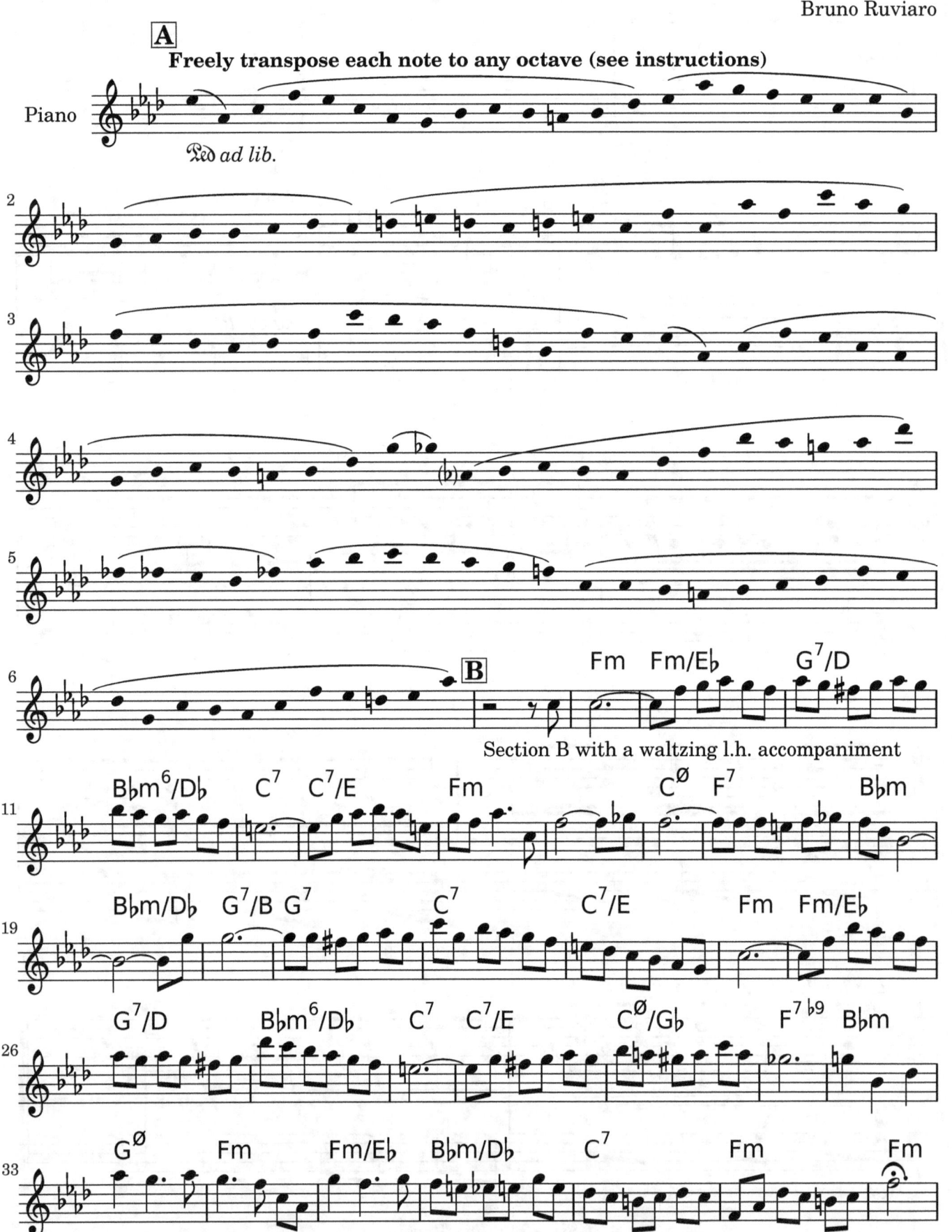

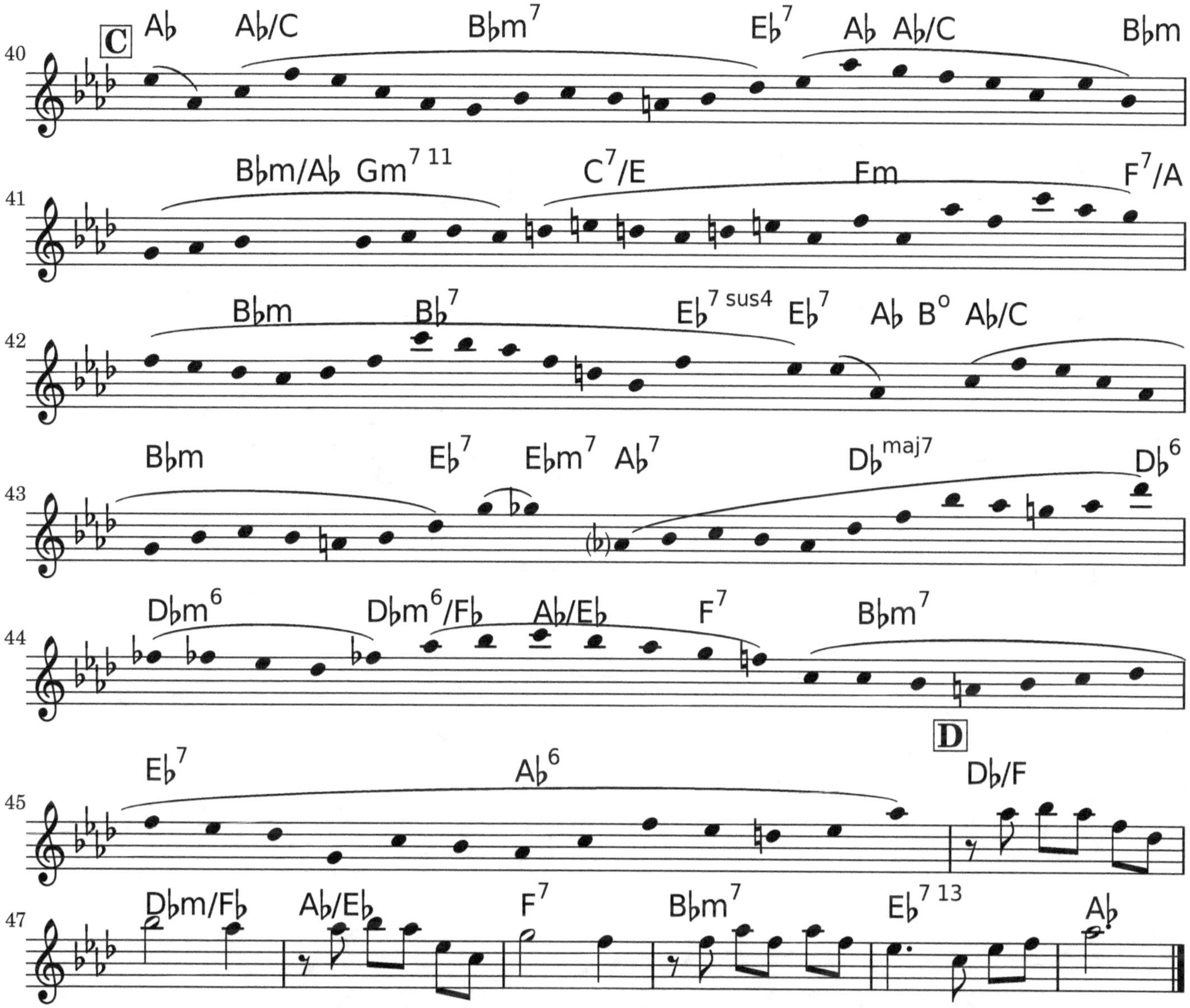

INSTRUCTIONS - The score of Pós-Tudo 8 is a guide for improvisation and arrangement, much like a lead sheet. Typical skills of a jazz pianist are expected, as well as modern free improv. The following guidelines apply:

1) Octave displacements: transpose each pitch of the melody to any desired octave of the piano. The interval between any two adjacent notes **must always be larger than a perfect fifth.** This rule applies to the melody of the entire piece, including the B section with left hand accompaniment. You can freely split melodic notes between right hand and left hand as needed.

2) You can freely choose the duration of stemless notes (sections A and C).

3) Phrasing slurs are optional and can be used to influence your arrangement in any way.

4) In section B, the left hand introduces a waltz-like accompaniment with the indicated chords. The right hand continues the same process of octave transposition as before, only now the rhythms are written out. You may optionally choose to constrain your right hand to octaves that are above the notes played by your left hand.

5) Section C is similar to section A but with added harmonies. Amidst the melodic notes with octave transpositions, you should add hints of the indicated chords. You may use as few as one or two notes to merely suggest a chord, or you may use all notes of the chord to make a chord very explicit. Chords can be voiced in any way you like, including conventional jazz voicings, but also less conventional ones. Chords may be played as blocks (all notes simultaneously), or scattered around melodic notes. Not all chords necessarily need to be played.

6) Section D is a coda. It can be played like section B, with perhaps less disjunct octave displacements (i.e., the perfect fifth requirement from #1 can be relaxed, revealing a bit more of the original contour.)

[*Rosa*, Pixinguinha]

Pós-Tudo 10

Bruno Ruviaro

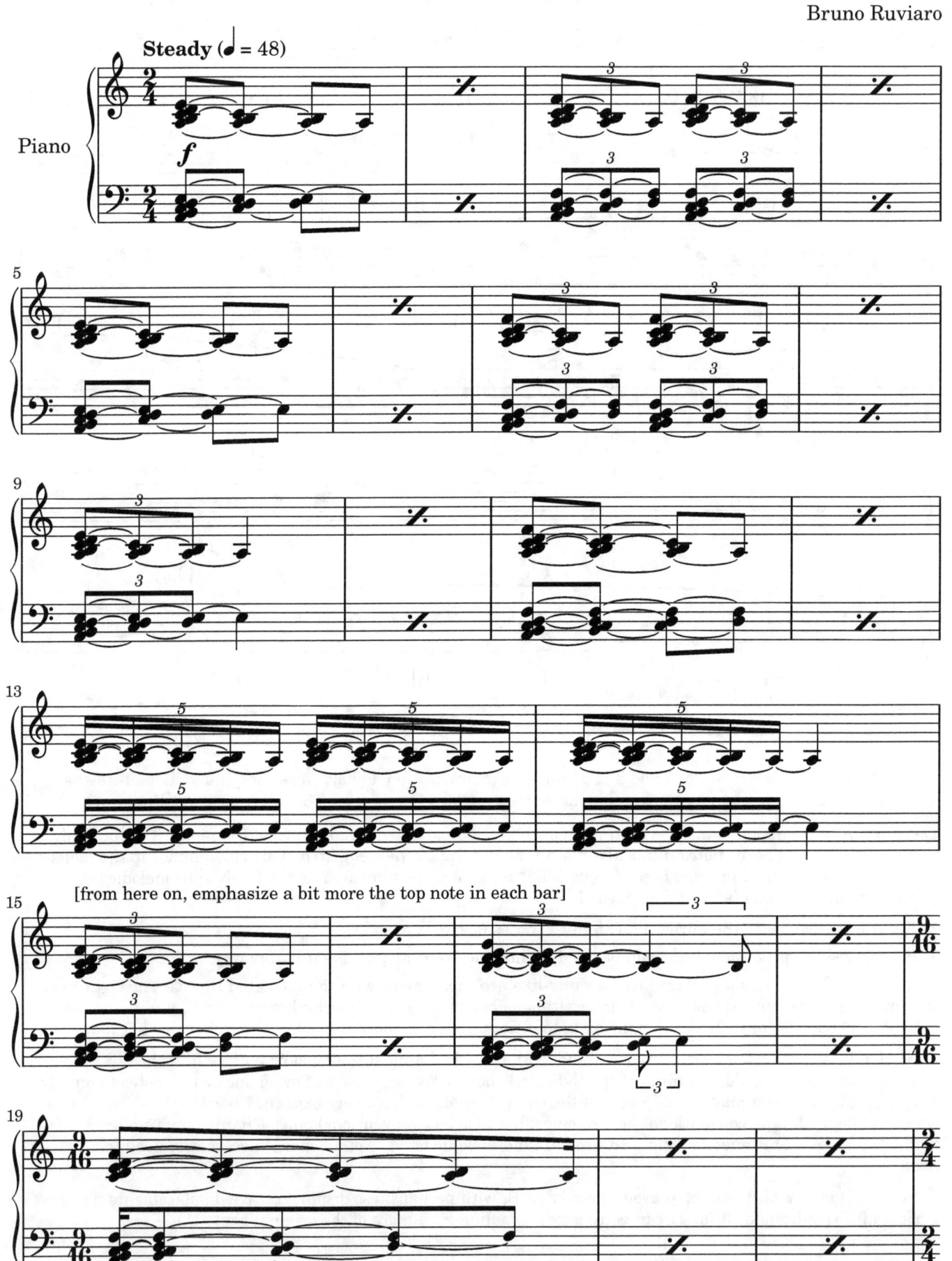

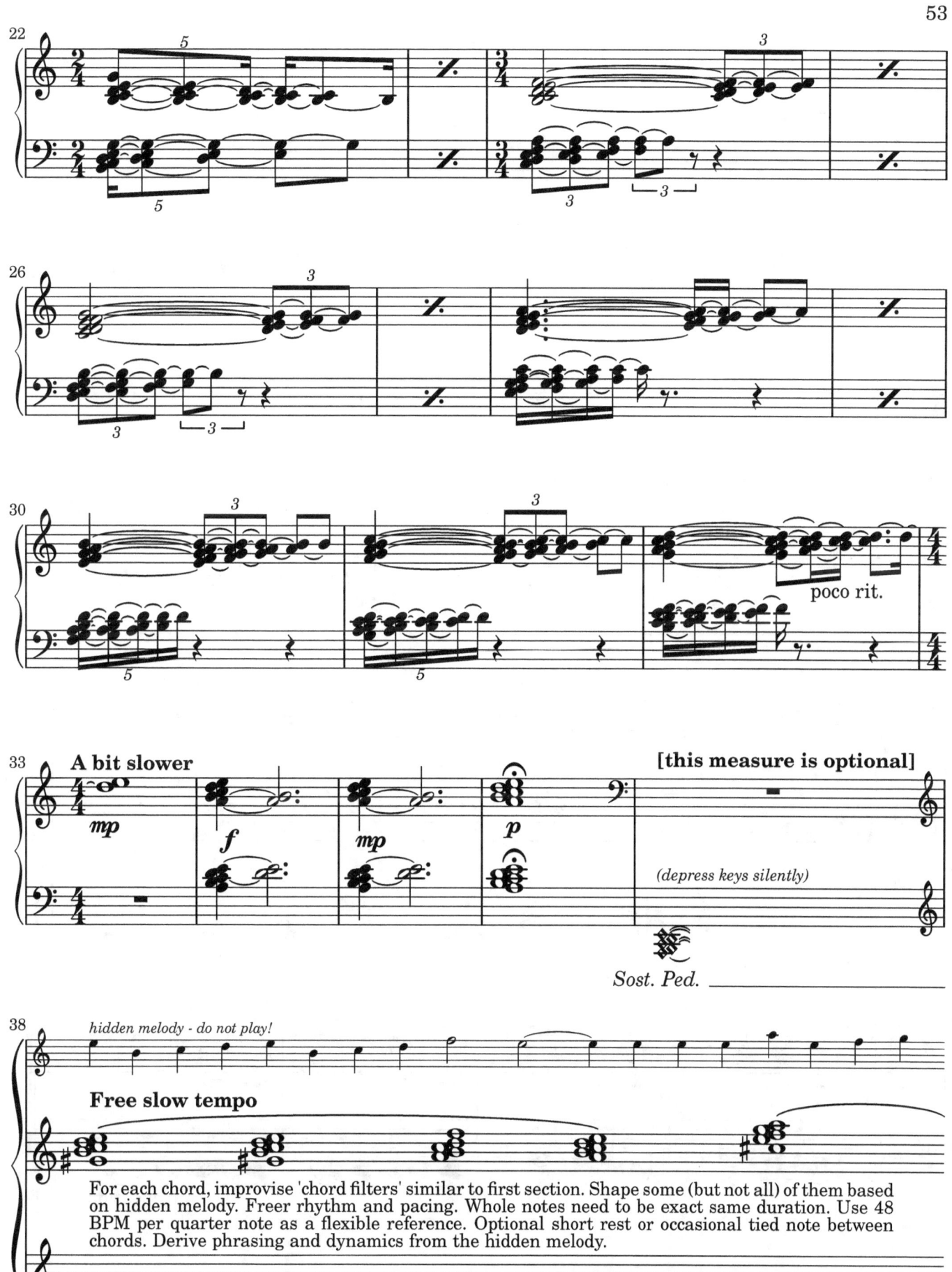

A bit slower

[this measure is optional]

(depress keys silently)

Sost. Ped. _____

hidden melody - do not play!

Free slow tempo

For each chord, improvise 'chord filters' similar to first section. Shape some (but not all) of them based on hidden melody. Freer rhythm and pacing. Whole notes need to be exact same duration. Use 48 BPM per quarter note as a flexible reference. Optional short rest or occasional tied note between chords. Derive phrasing and dynamics from the hidden melody.

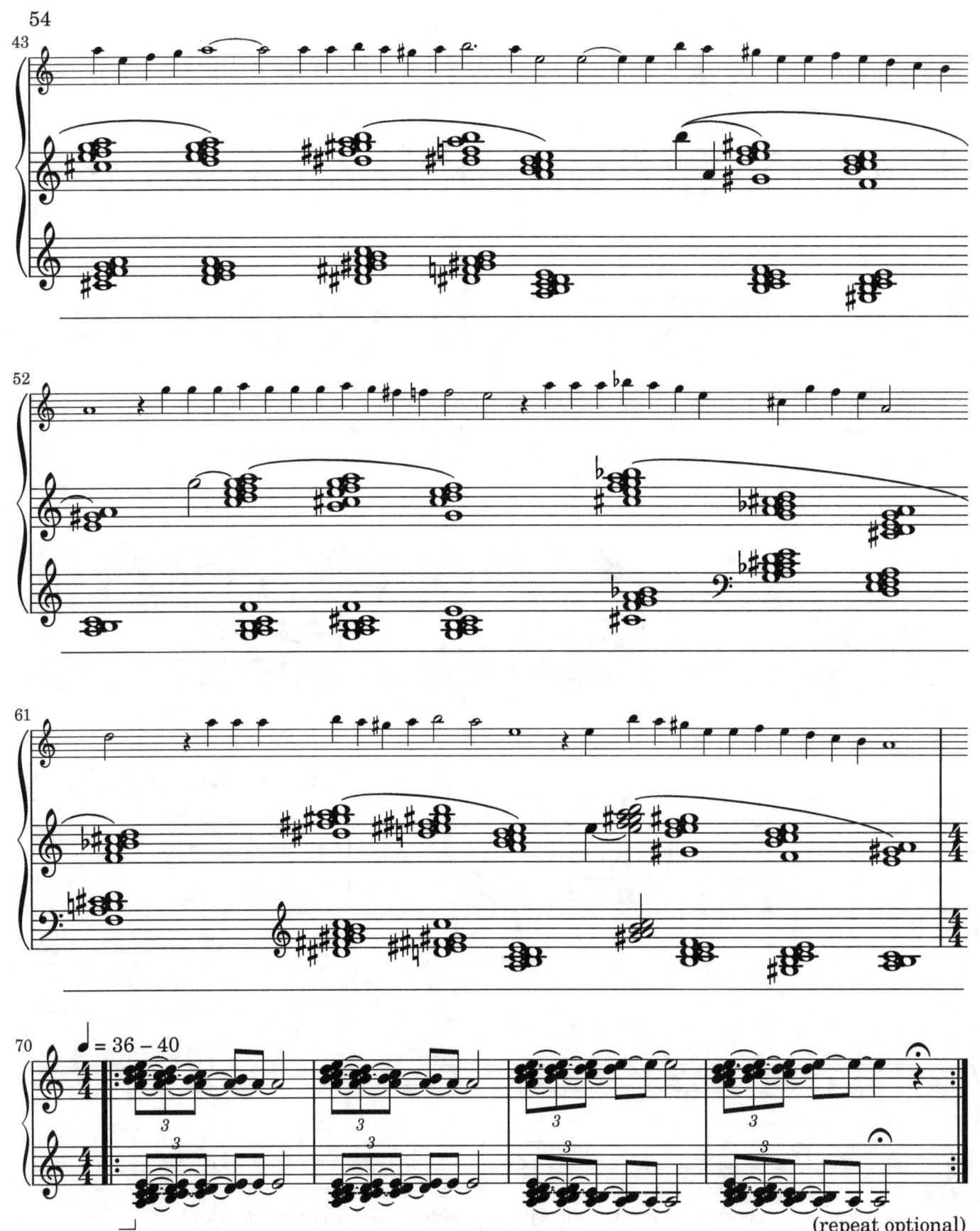

[*Lua Branca*, Chiquinha Gonzaga]

Pós-Tudo 11

for Teresa McCollough

Bruno Ruviaro

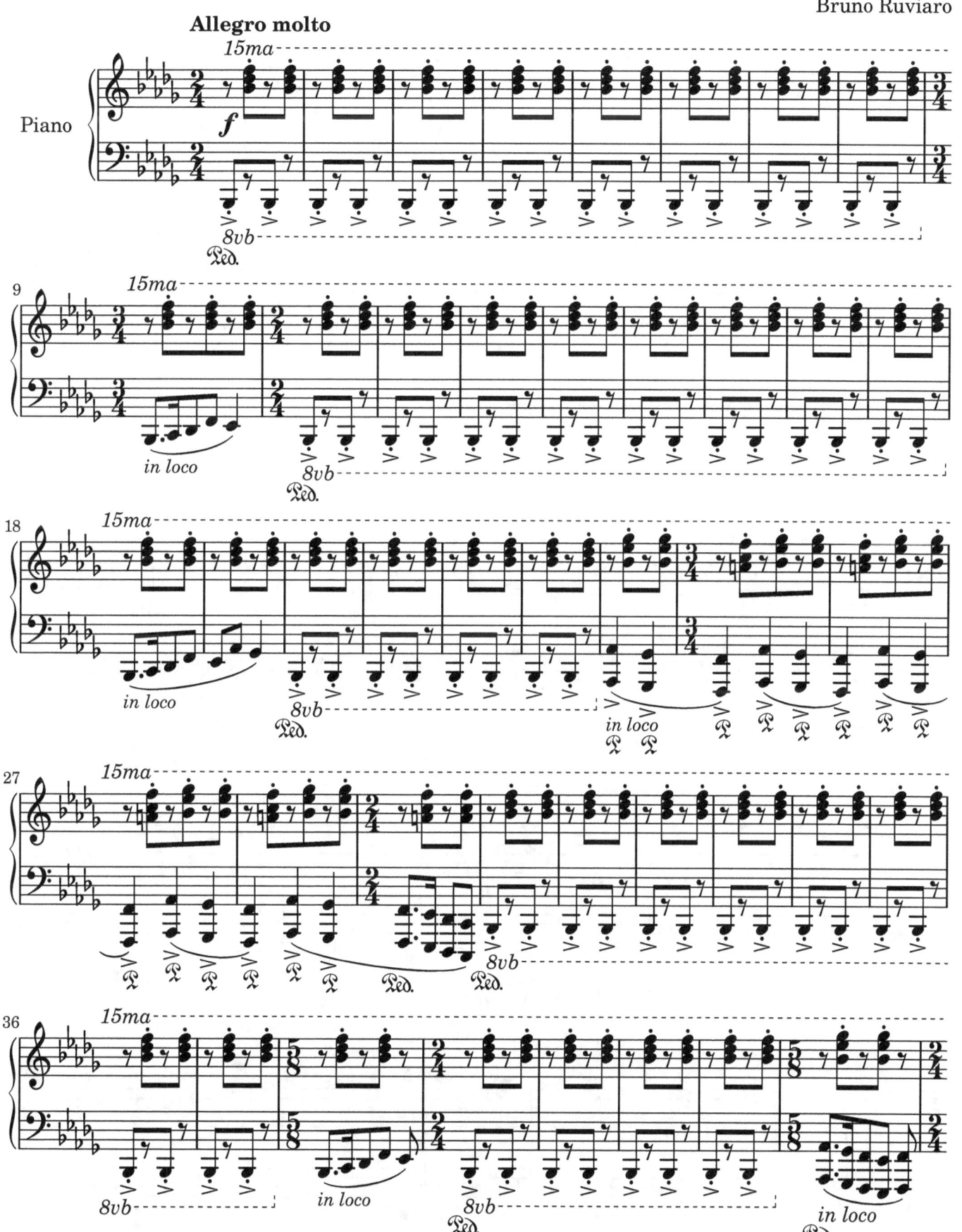

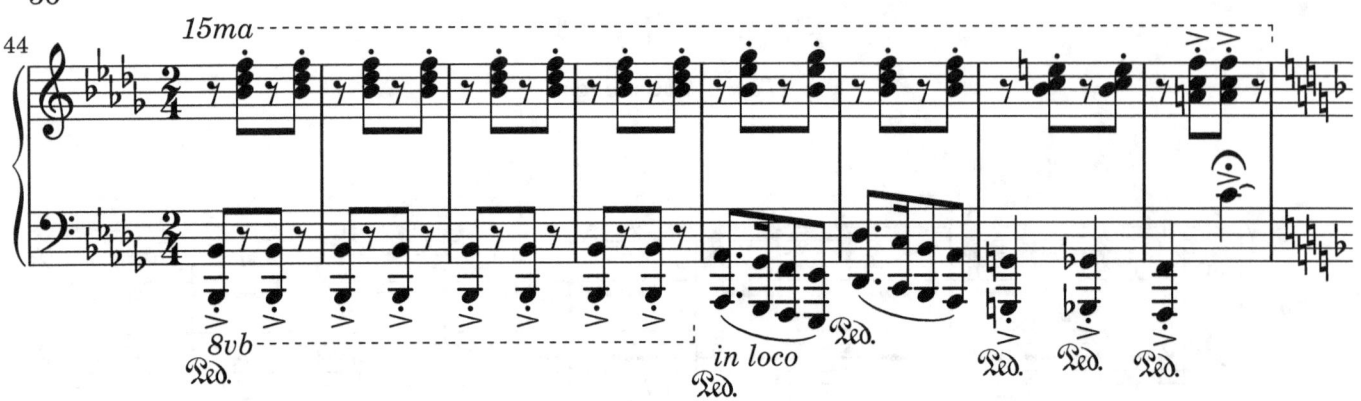

Slow or moderato

Wait about 4-5 seconds, then play any slow piano theme in F major that begins on the note C. It may be originally in F, or transposed to F. Examples: Beethoven Sonata Op. 2 Nr. 1, second movement; Schumann Reverie from Childhood Scenes; Schubert Impromptu in A flat major transposed to F; etc. It may also be a popular song. After about one or two full phrases, find a way to connect into next line and move on.

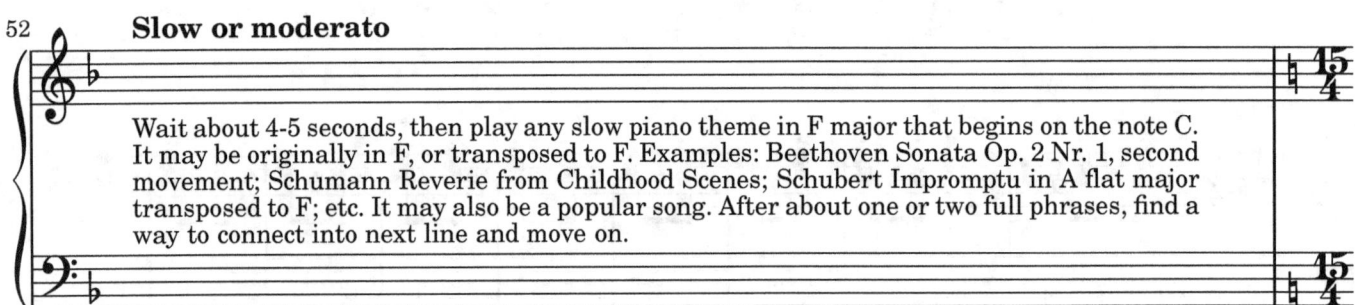

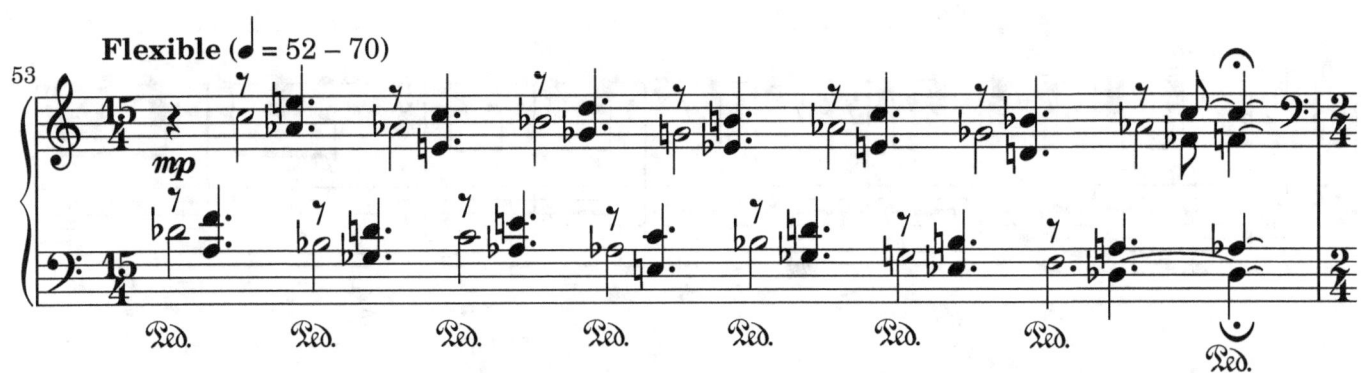

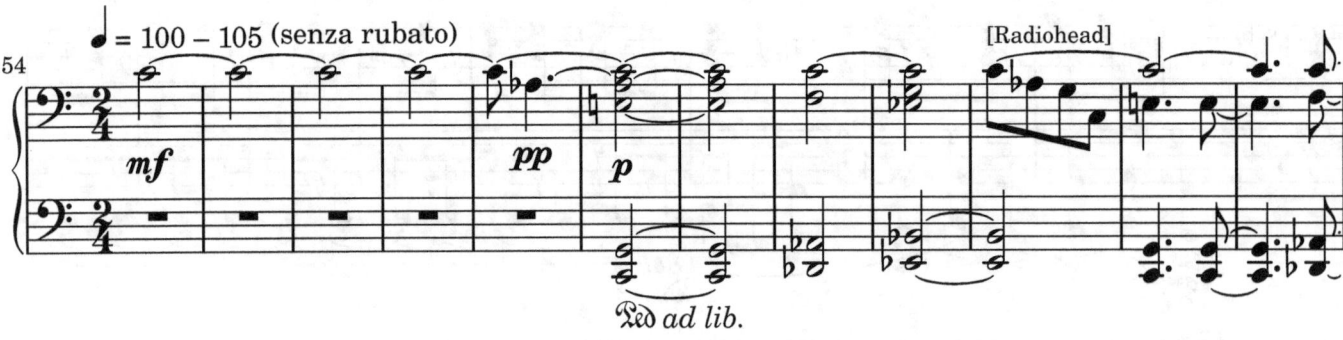

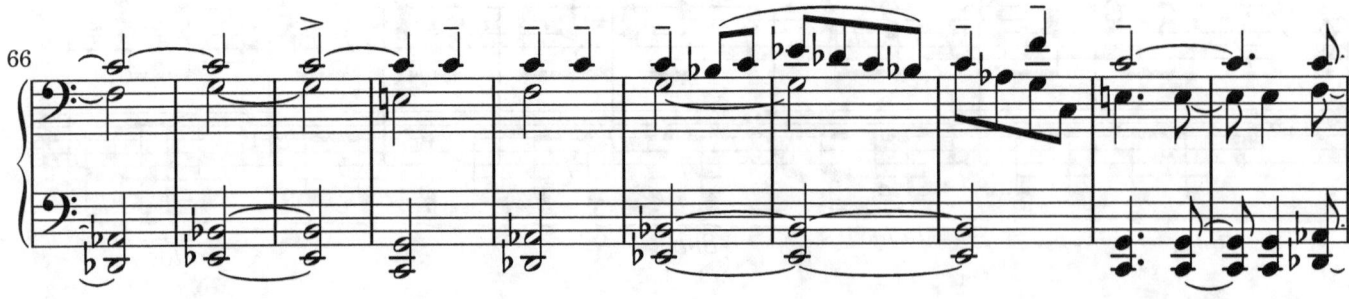

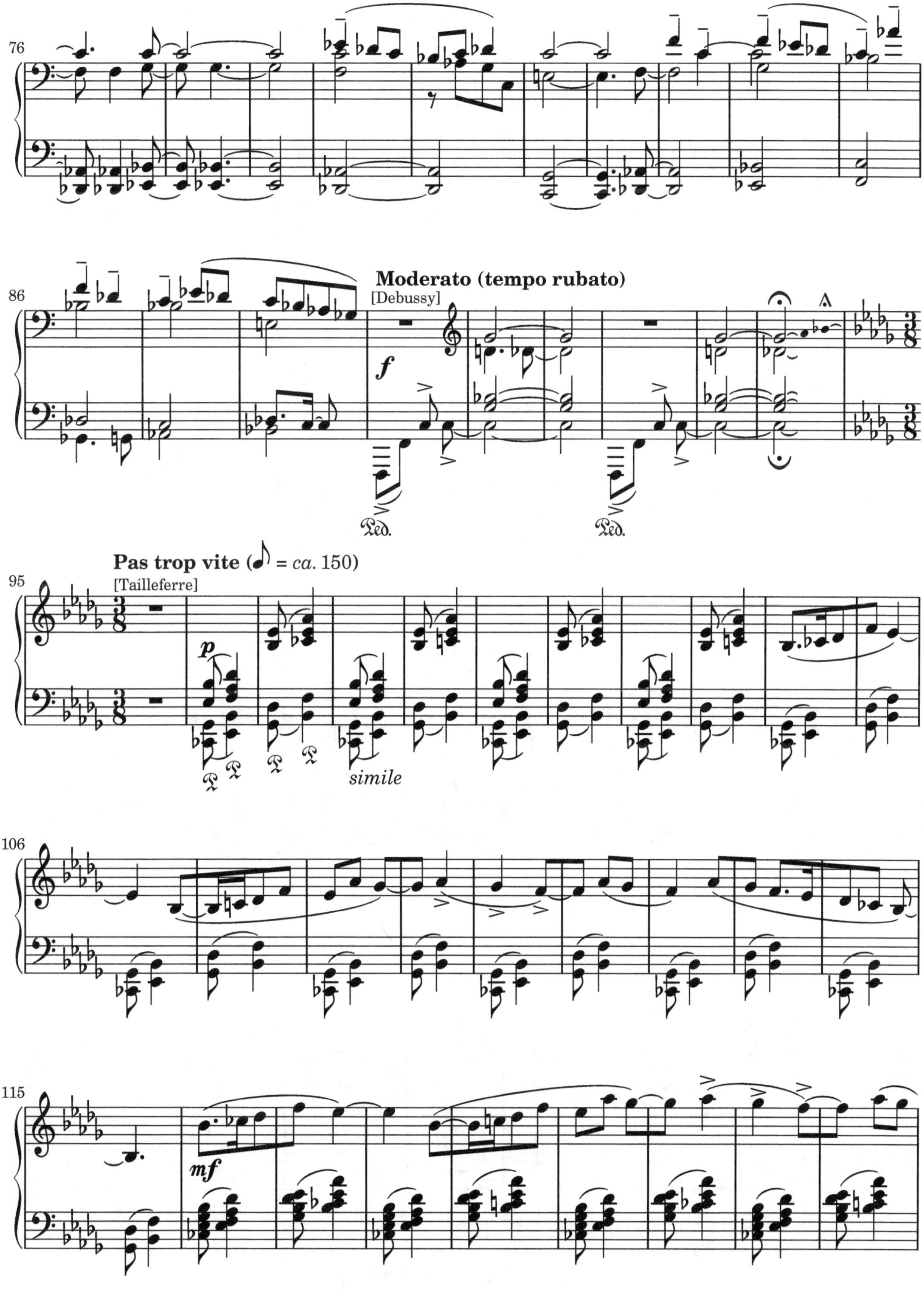

Moderato (tempo rubato)
[Debussy]

Pas trop vite (♪ = *ca.* 150)
[Tailleferre]

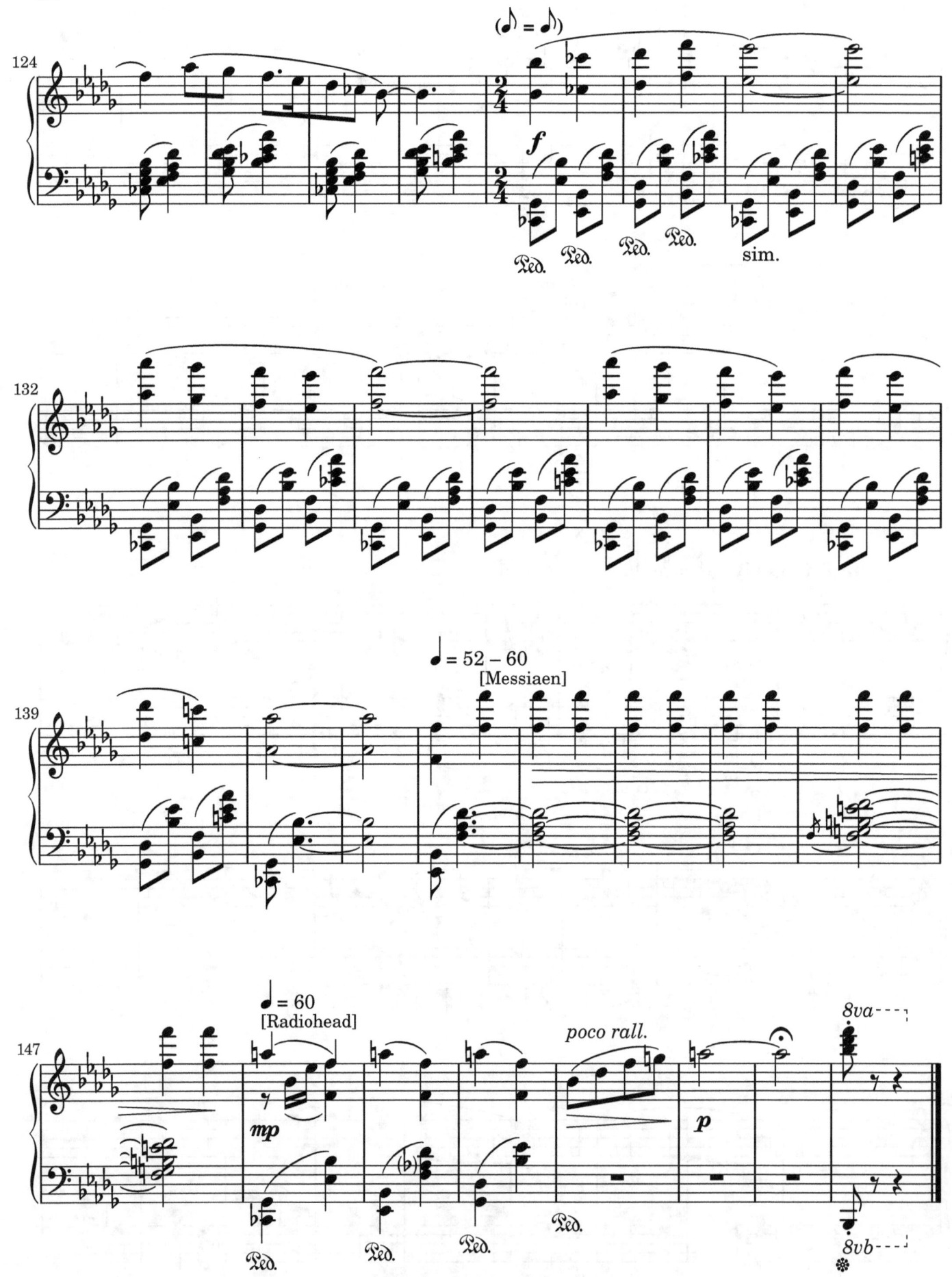

[*Op. 27, Nr. 29* , Kabalevsky]

Pós-Tudo 12

Bruno Ruviaro

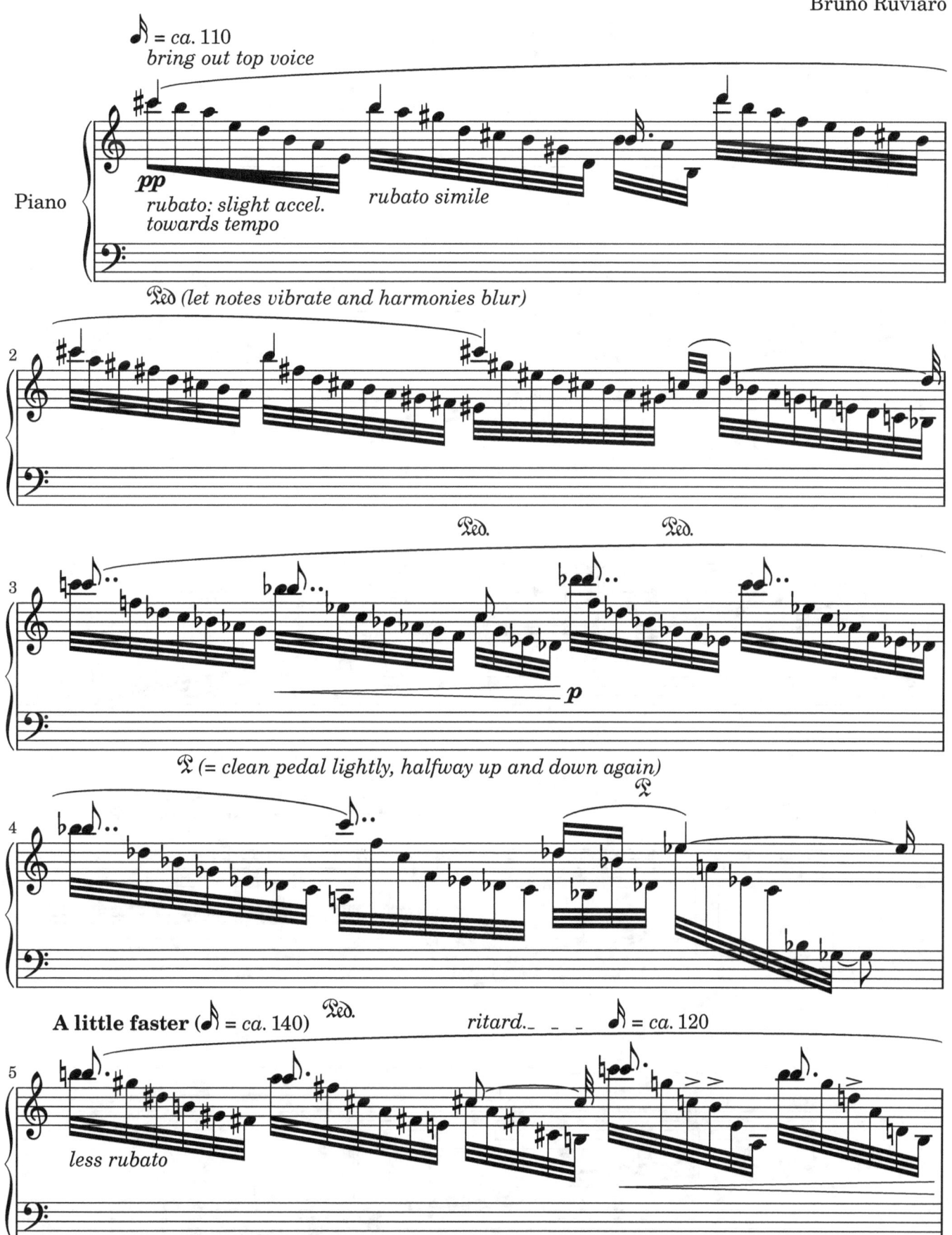

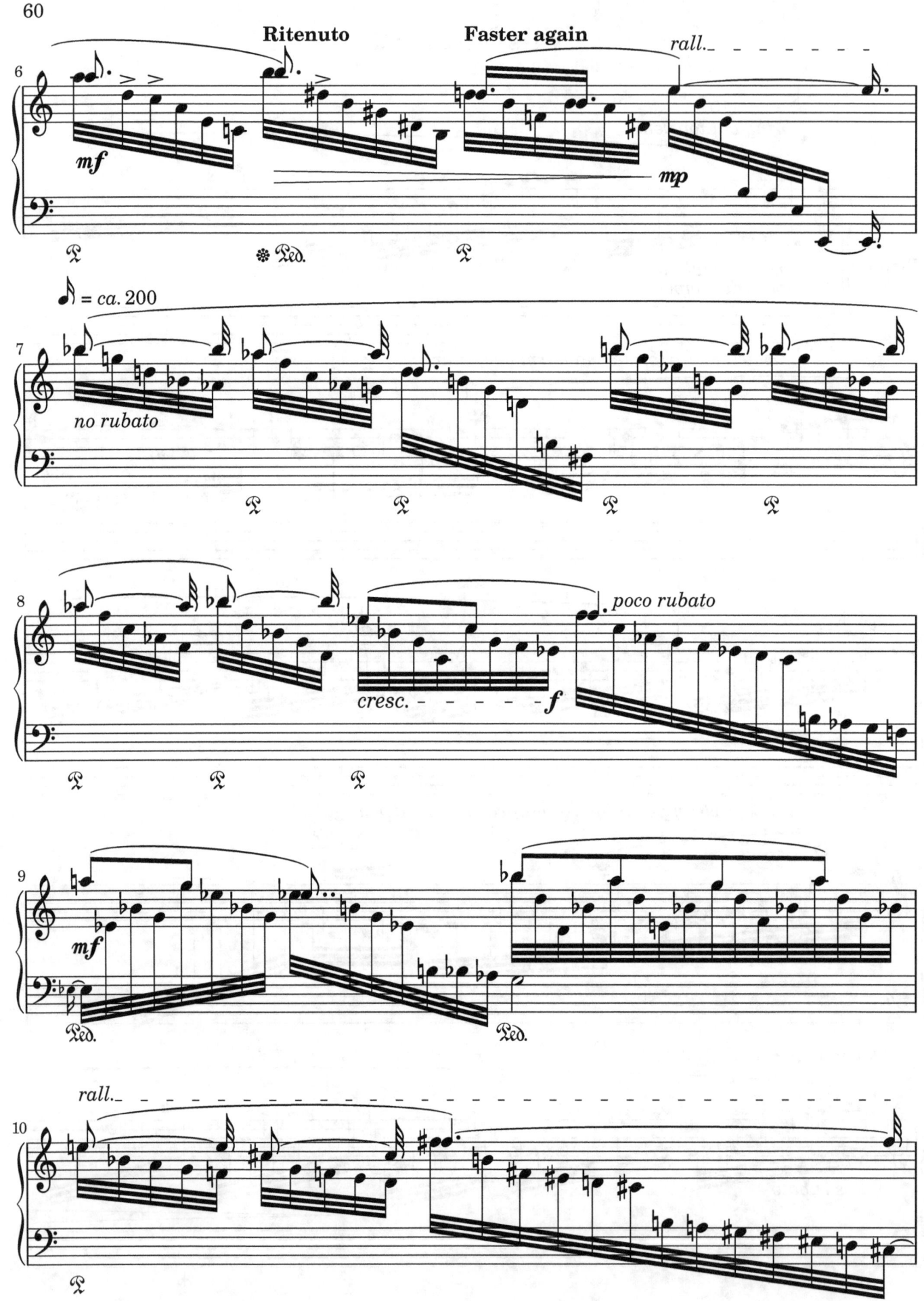

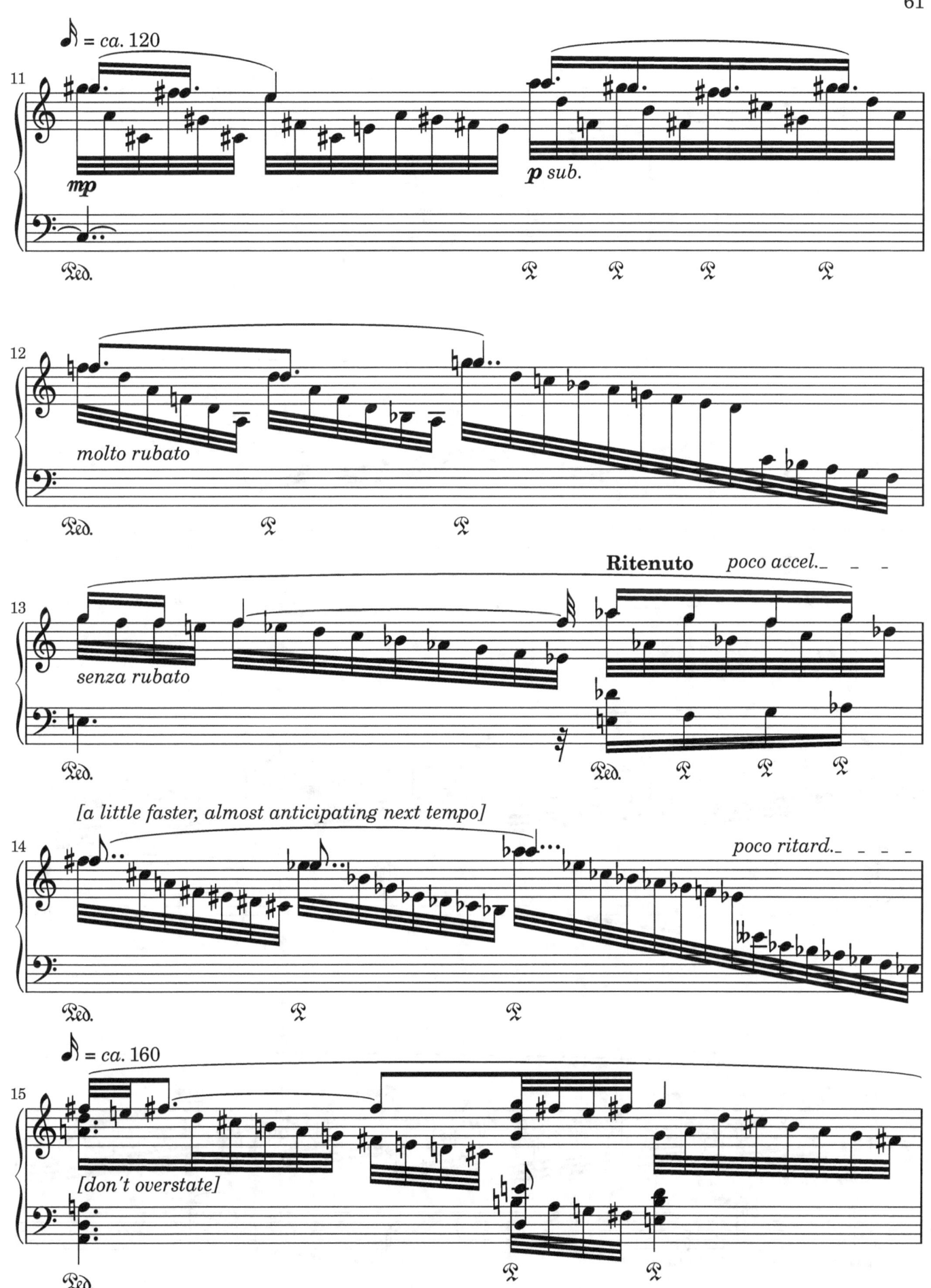

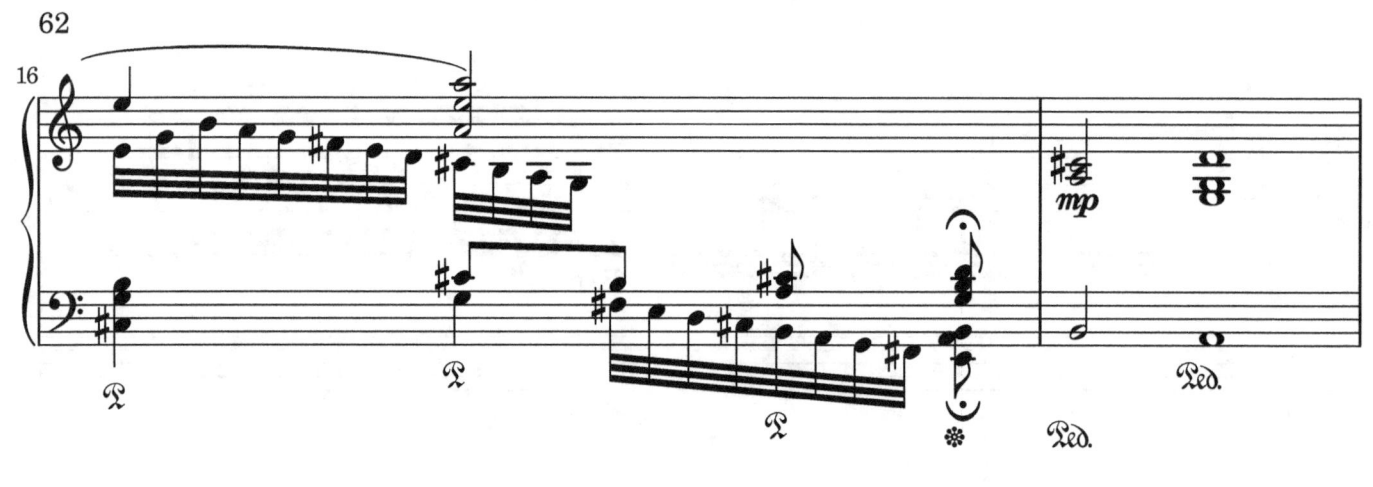

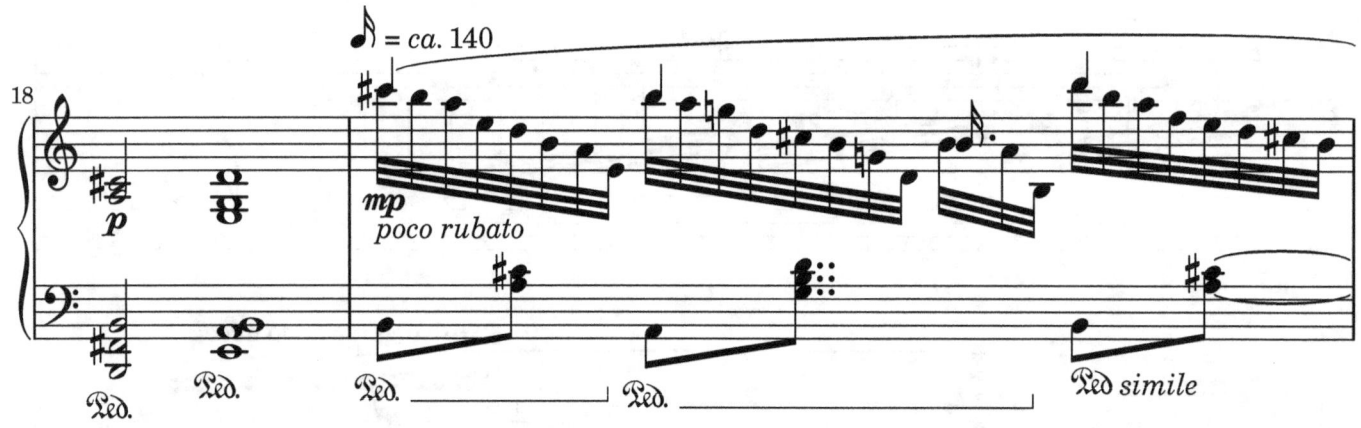

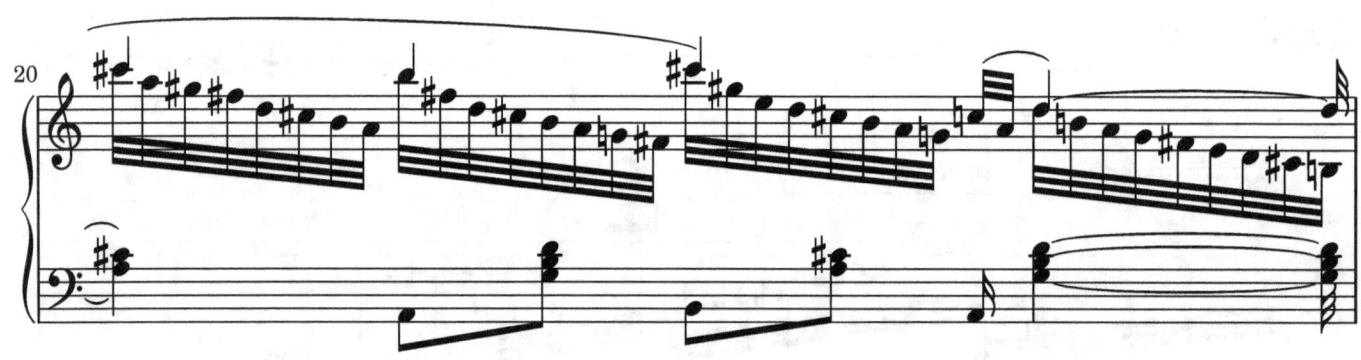

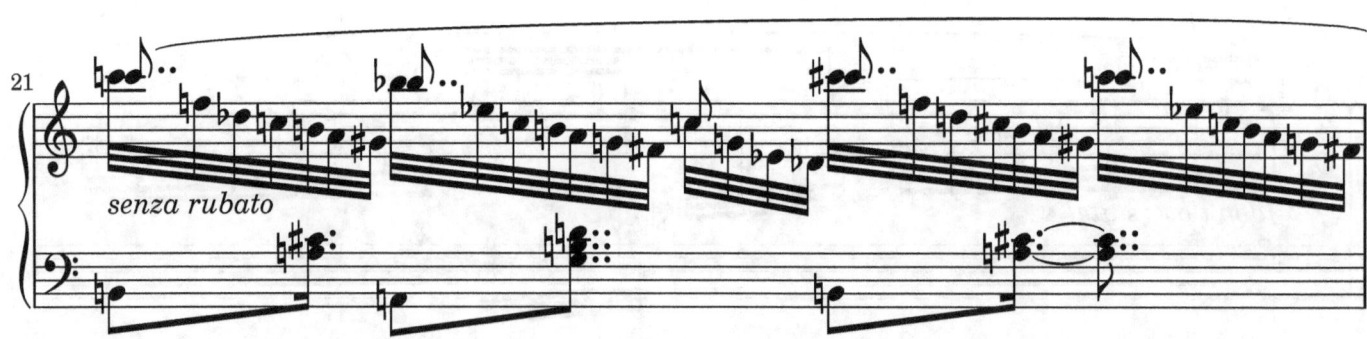

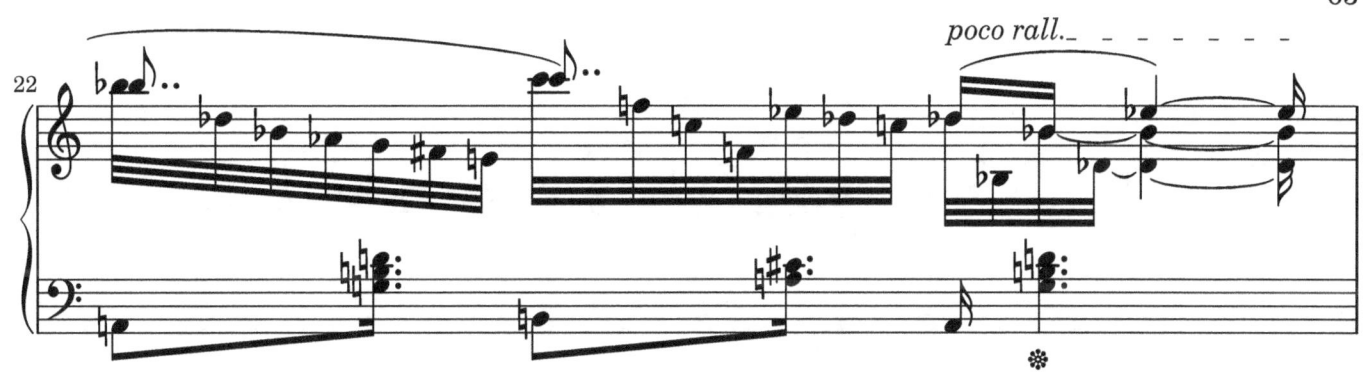

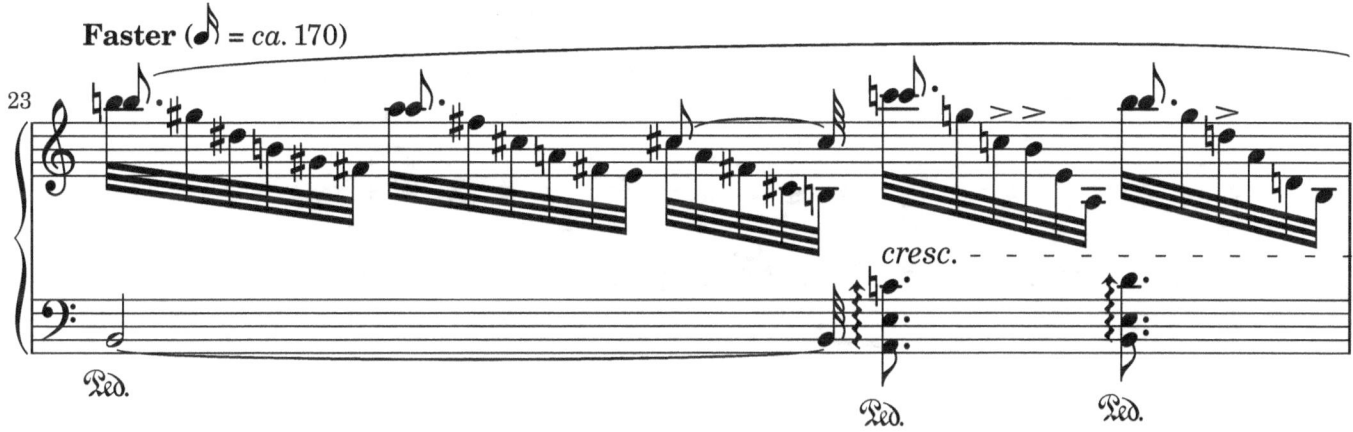

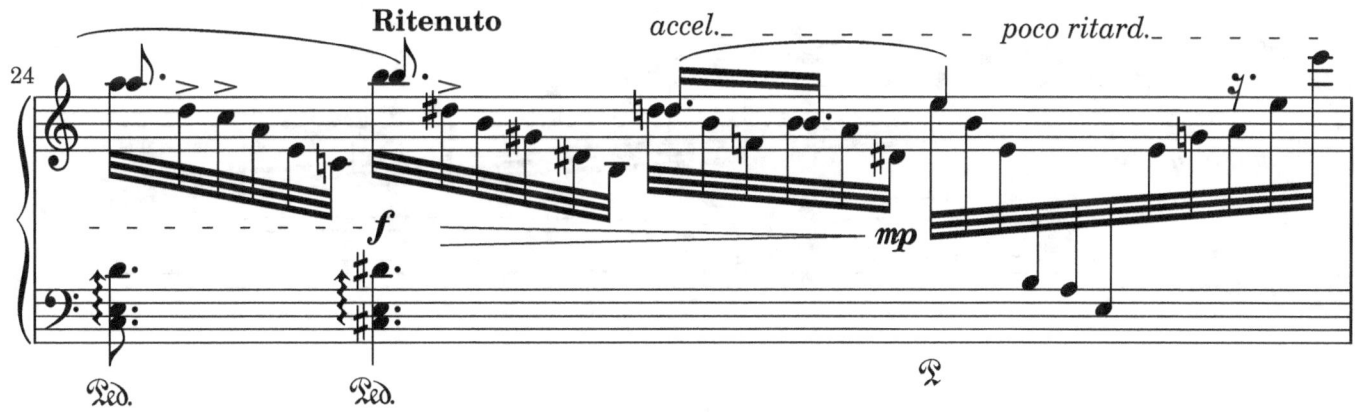

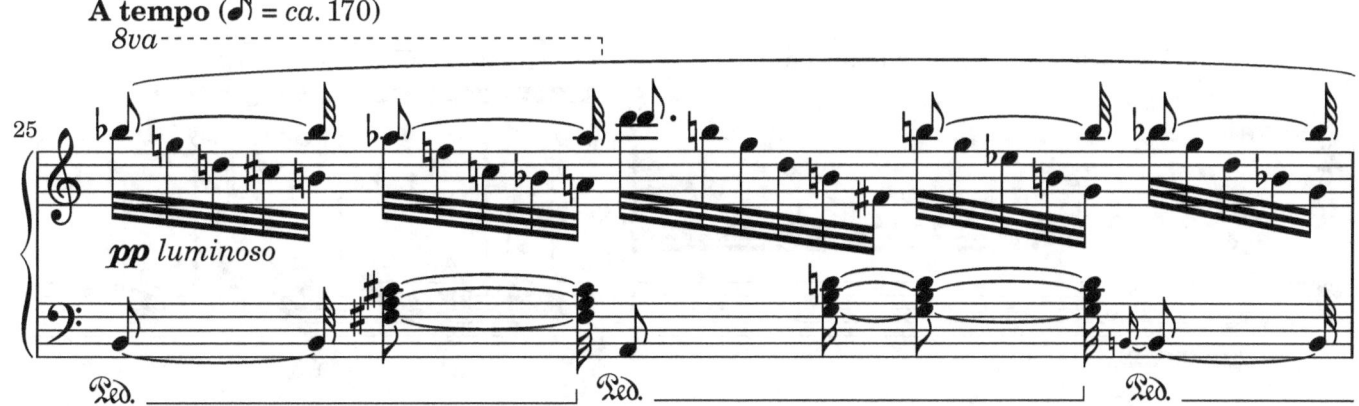

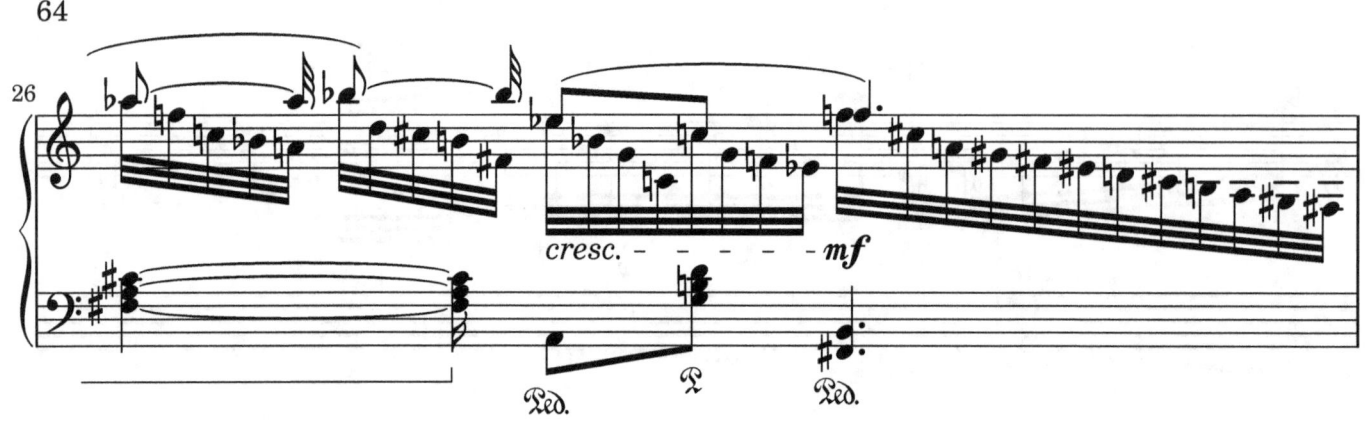

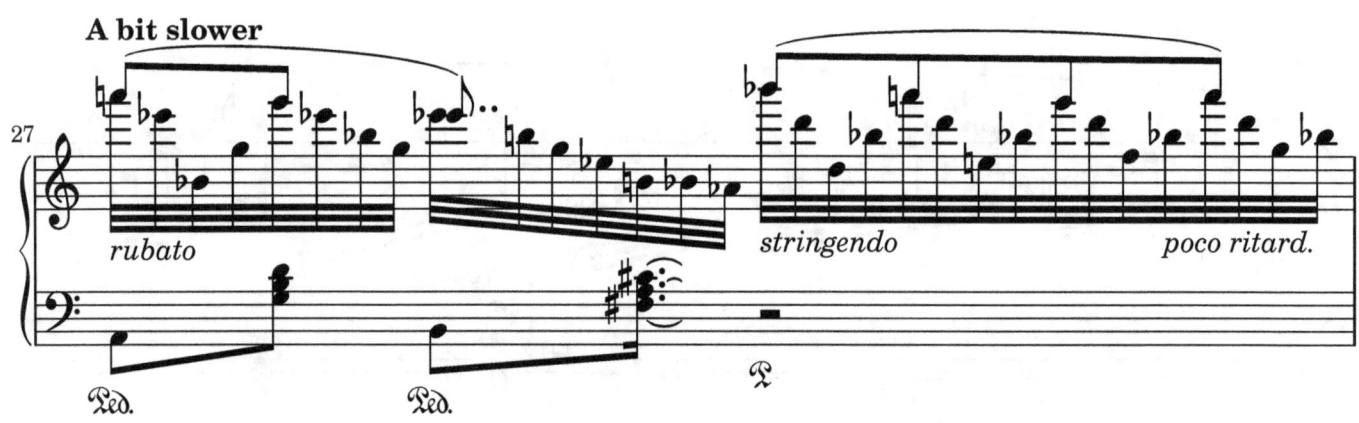

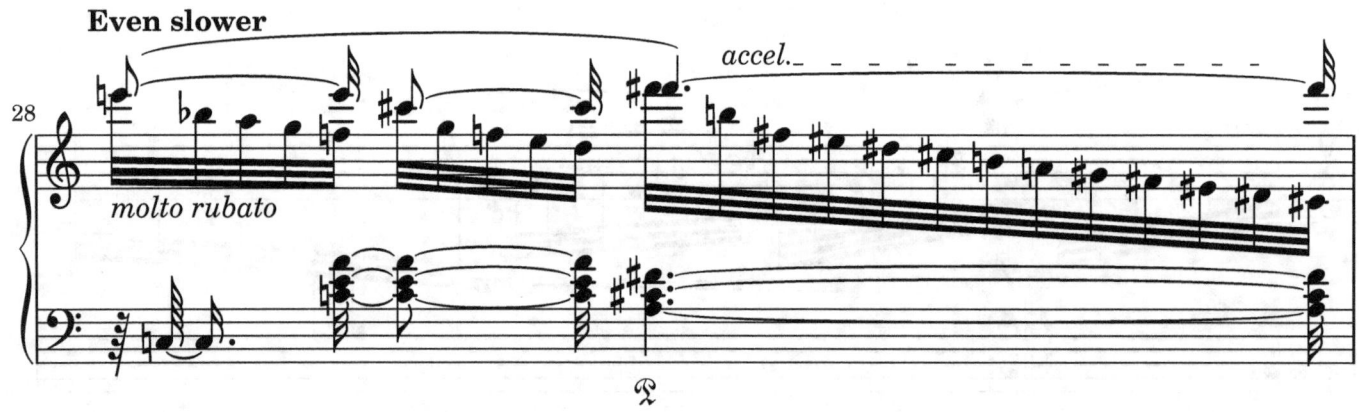

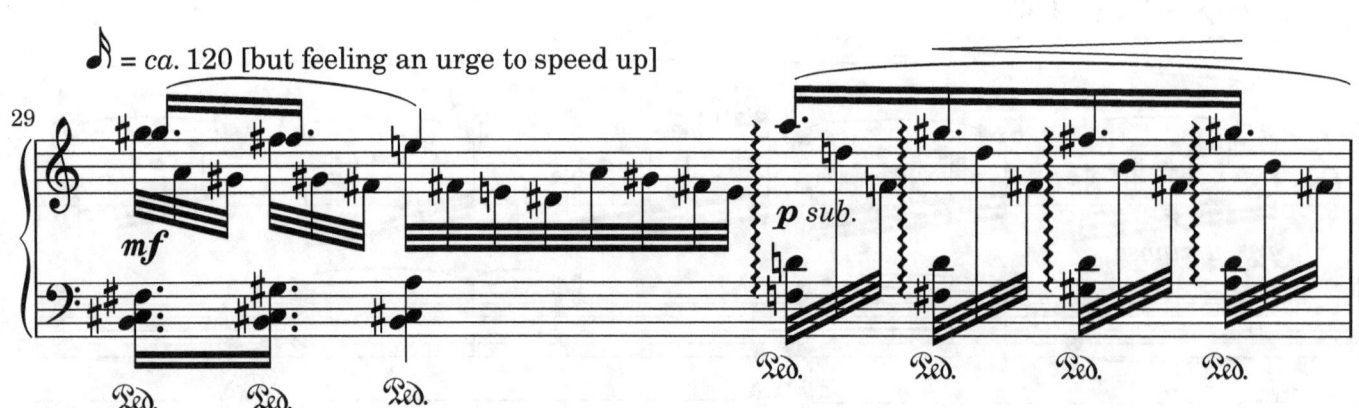

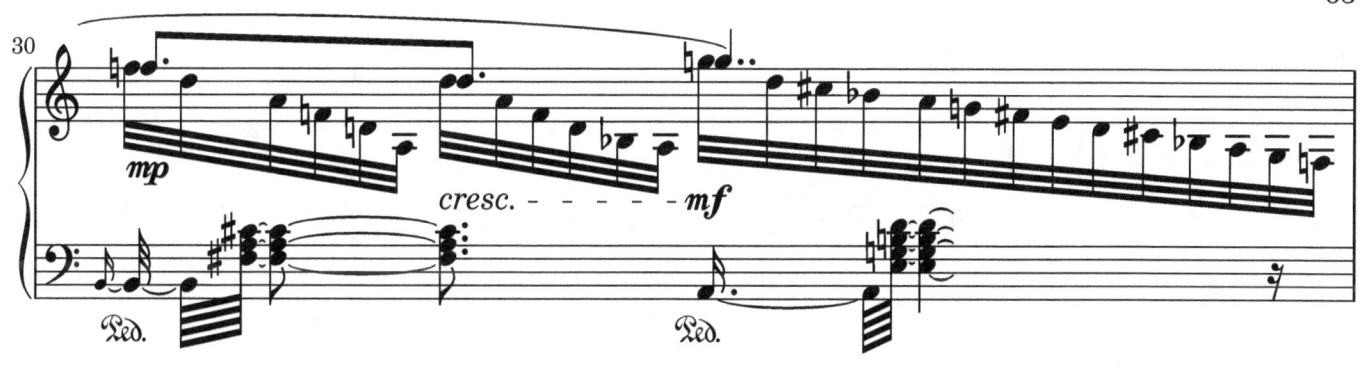

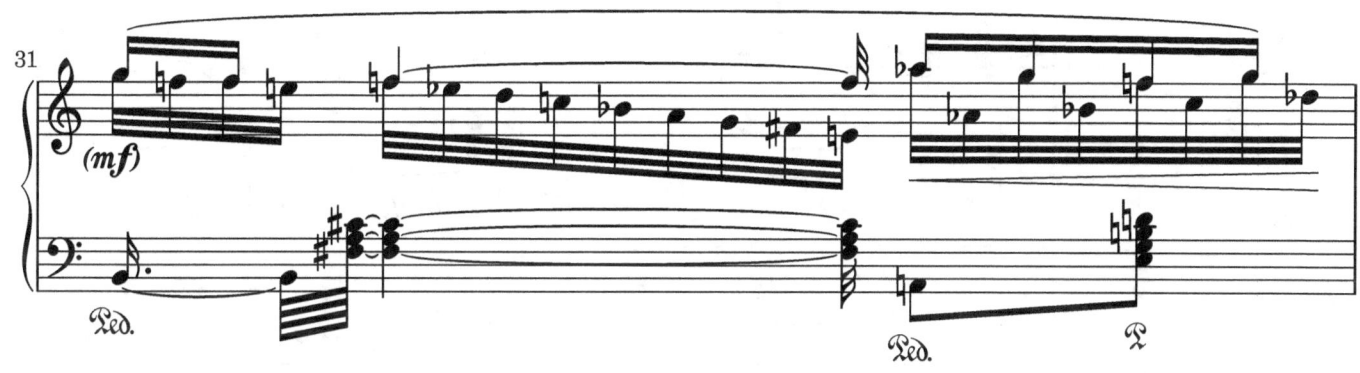

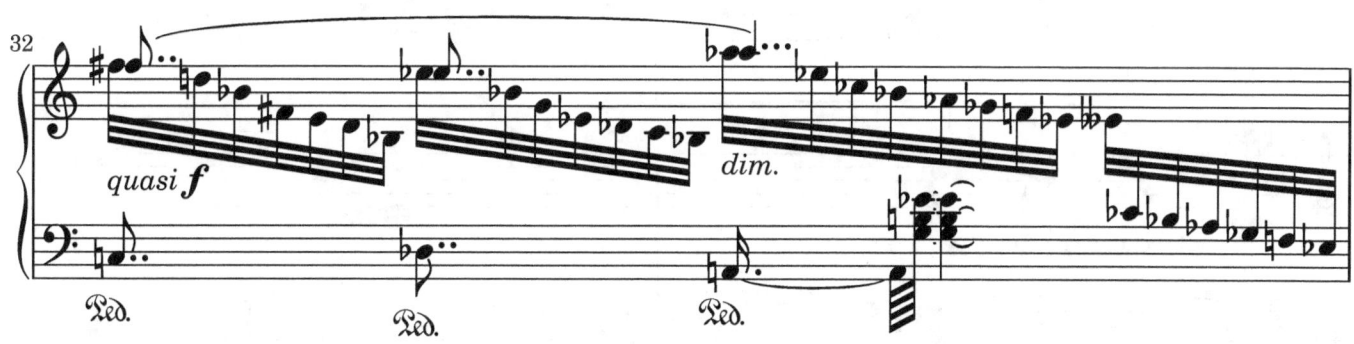

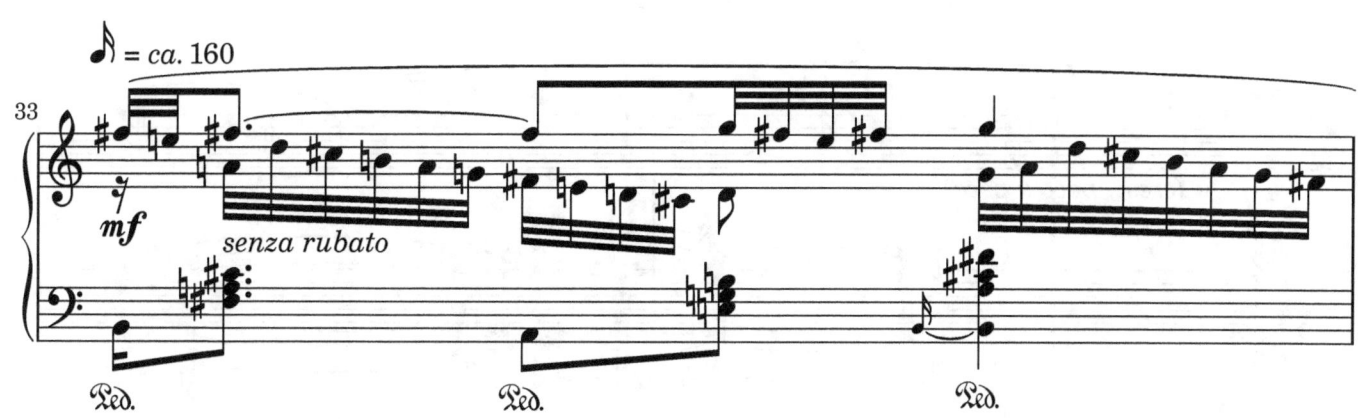

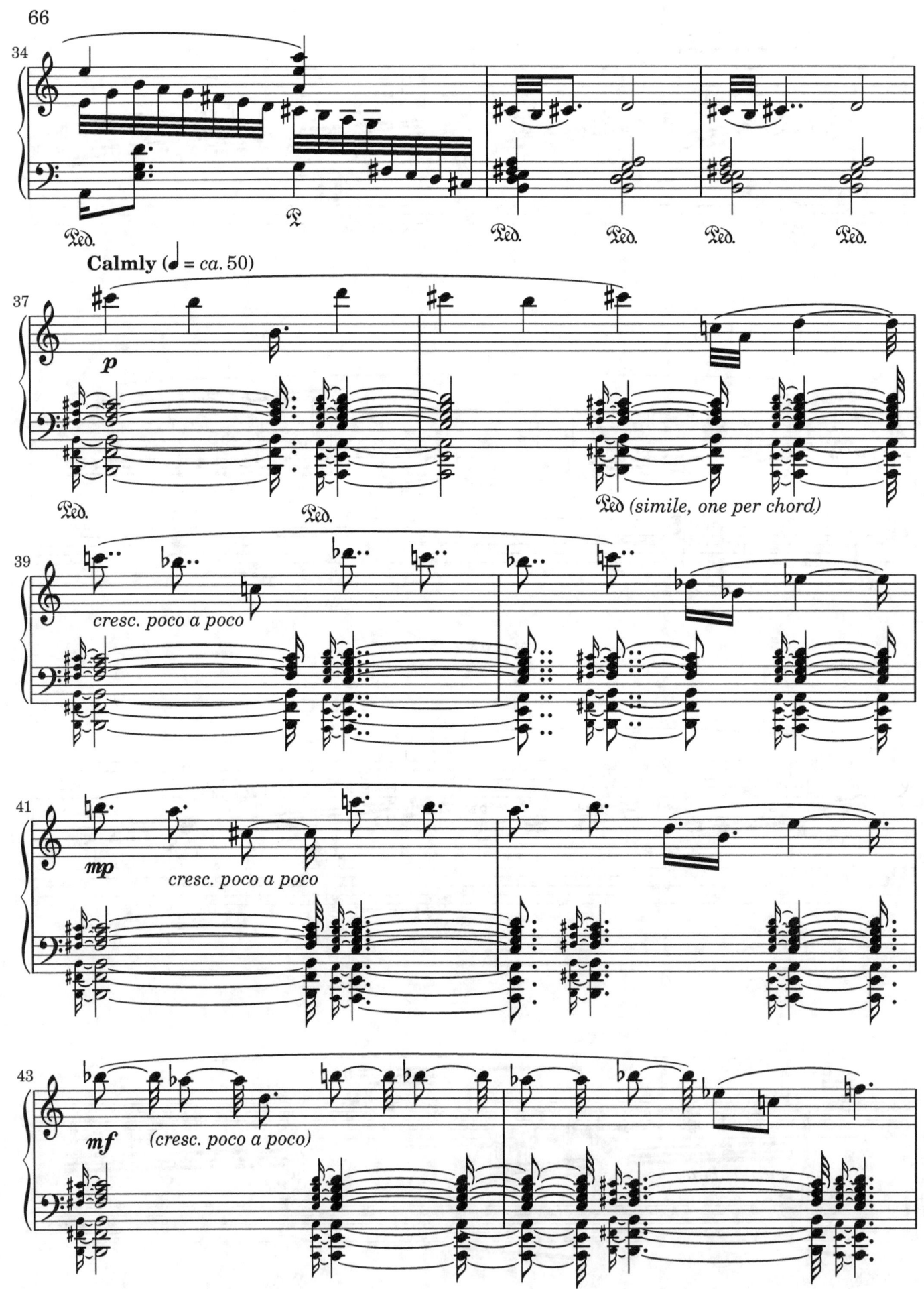

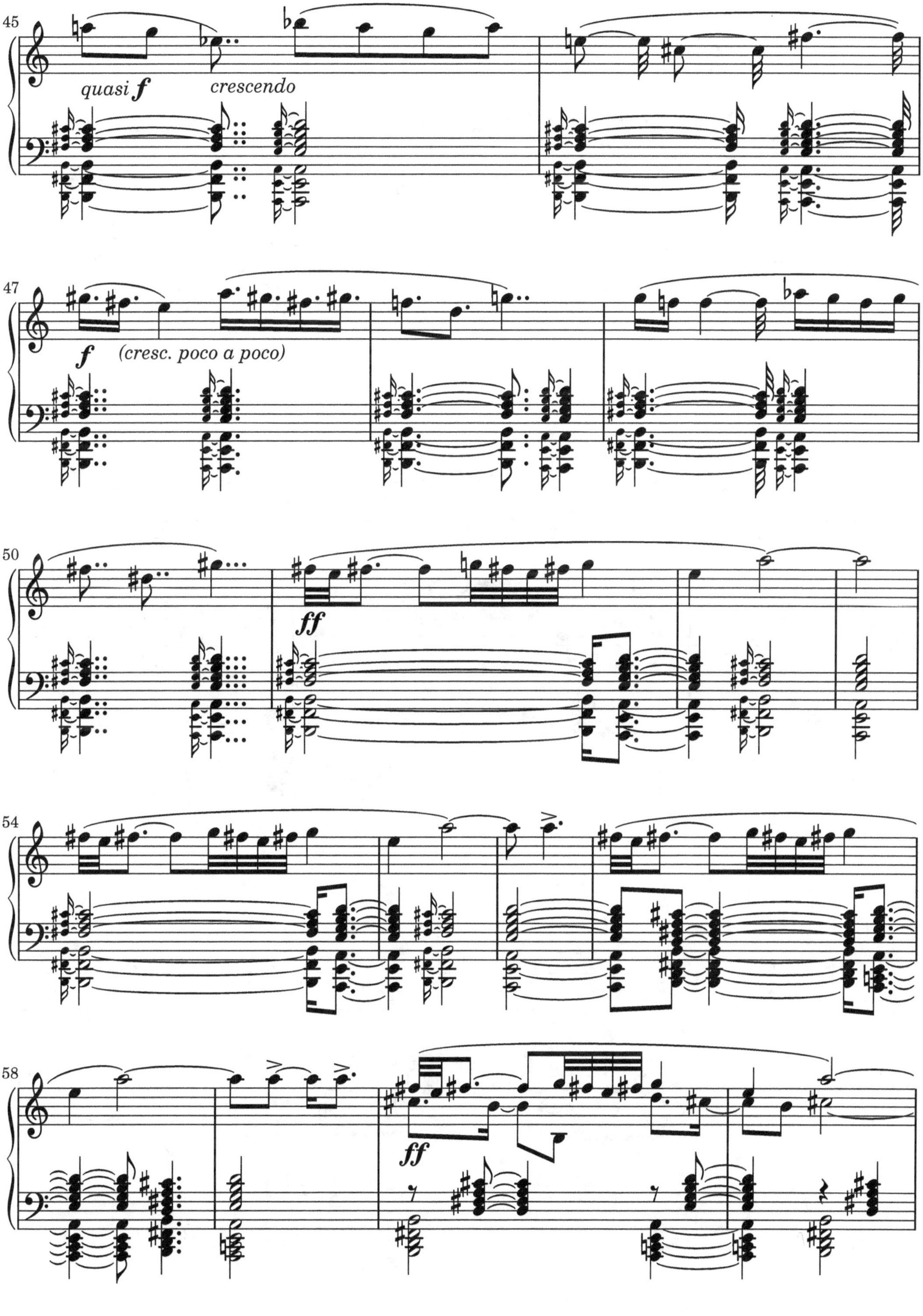

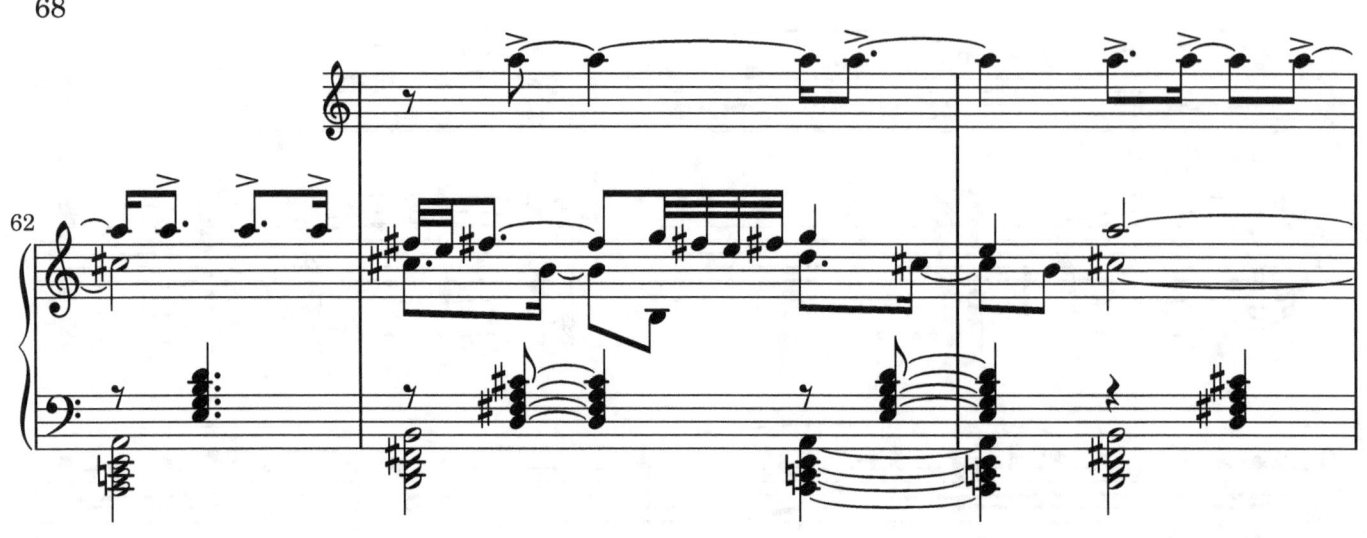

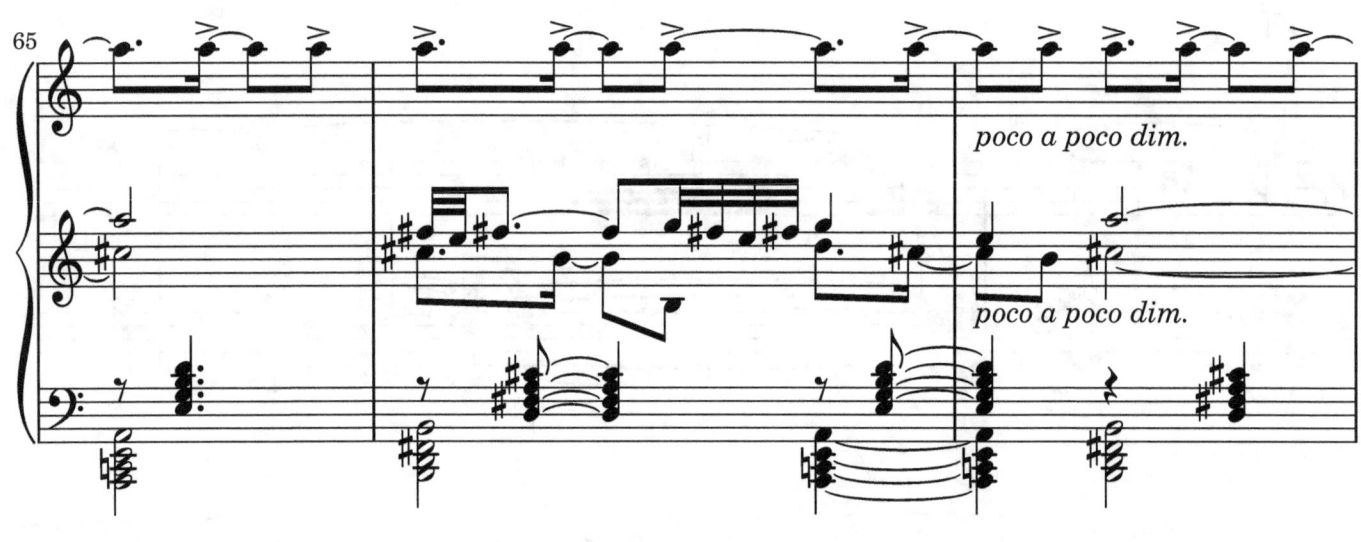

poco a poco dim.

poco a poco dim.

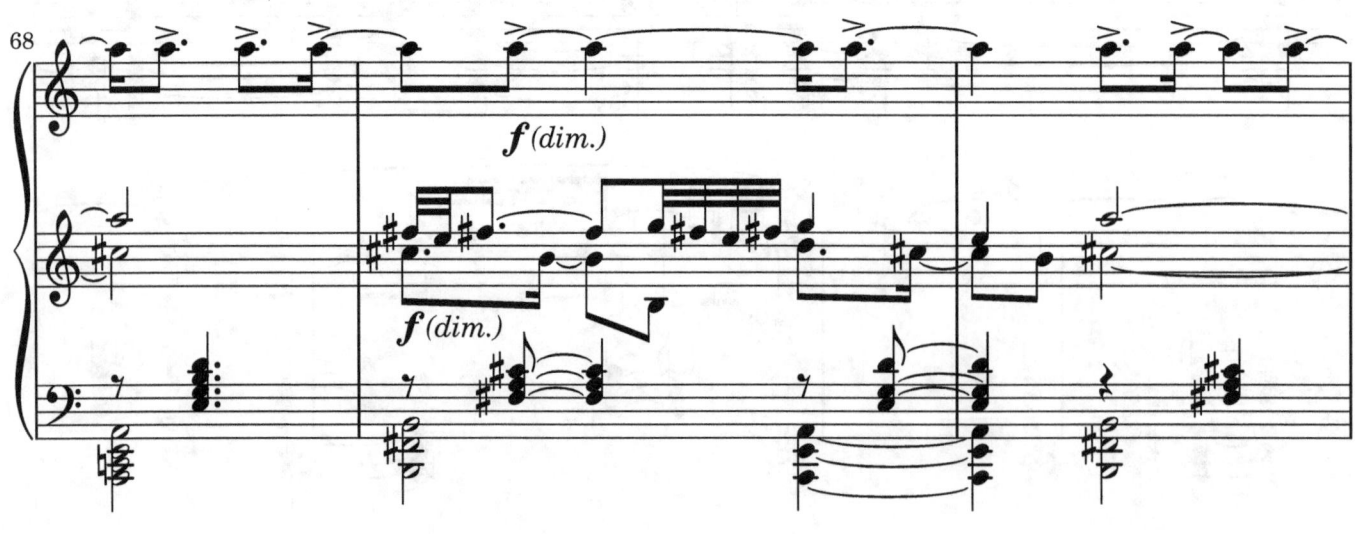

f (dim.)

f (dim.)

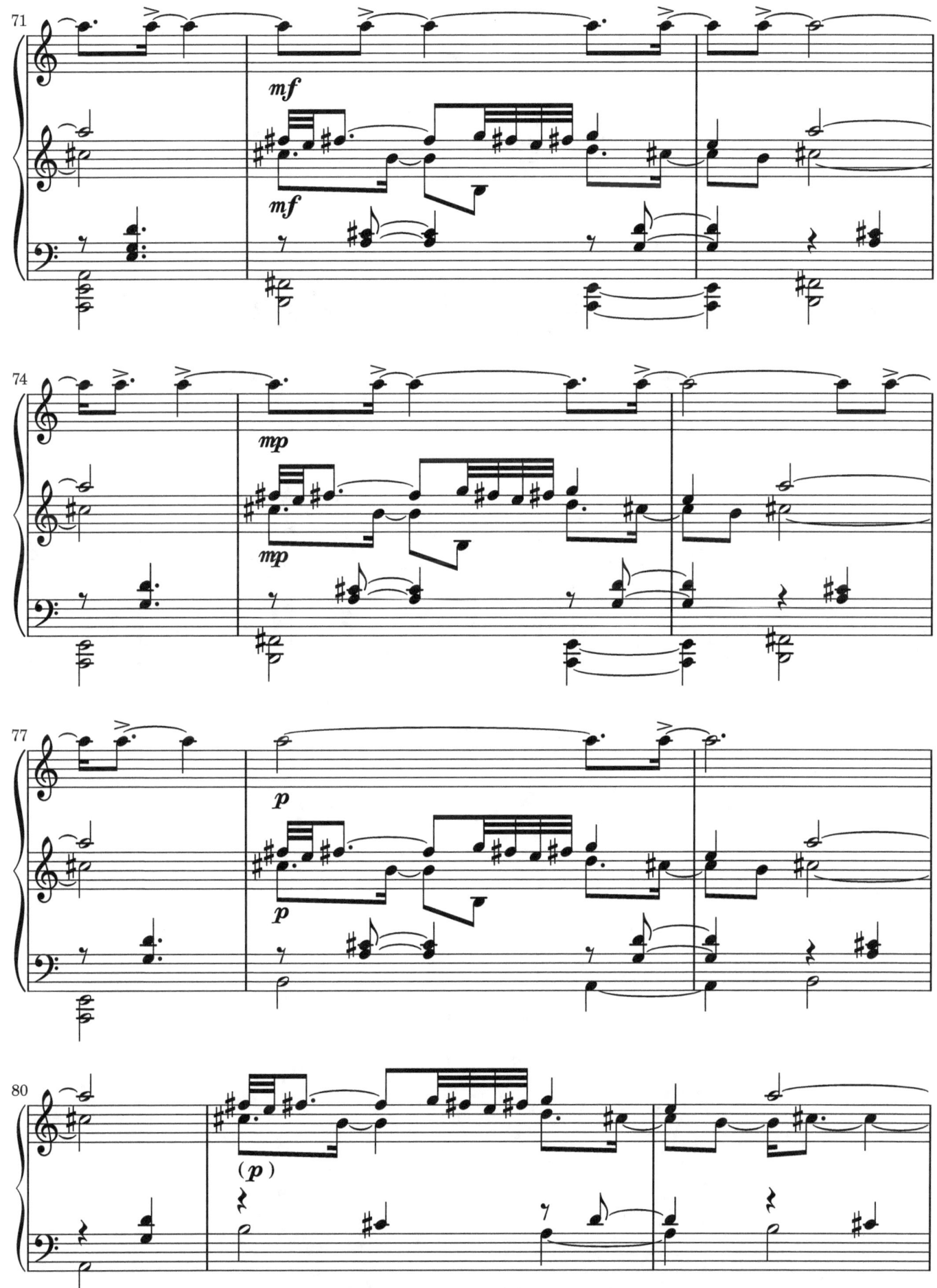

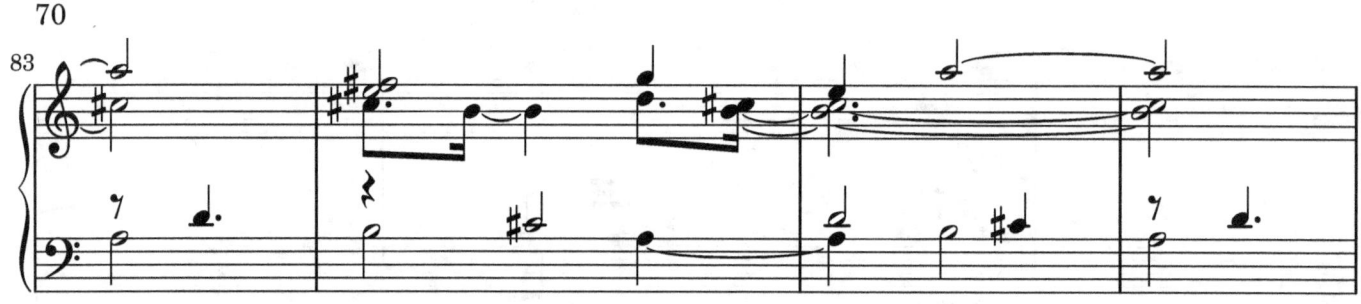

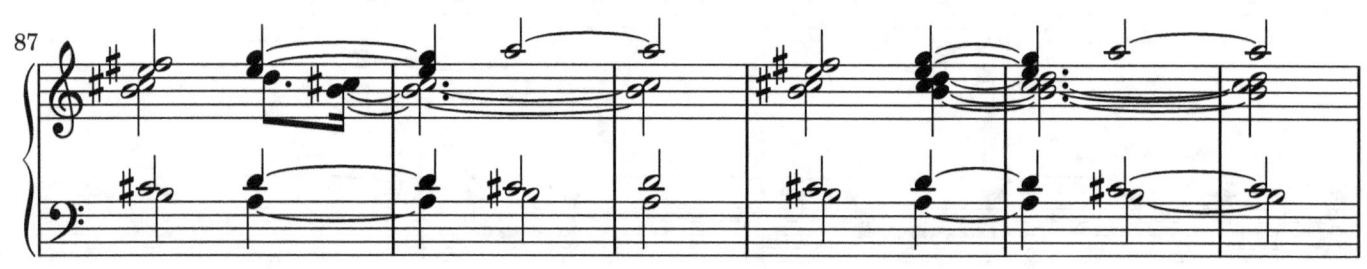

repeat a few times ad lib., fading out

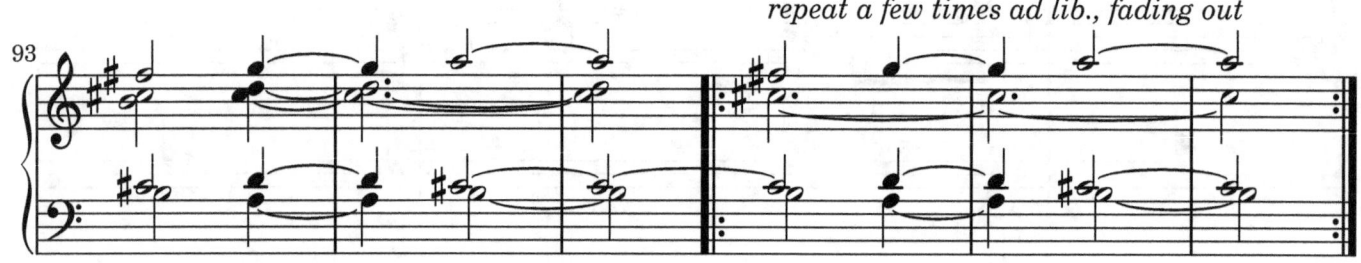

[*Partita in D, Menuet,* Bach]